THE
POLITICS
OF
RECONSTRUCTION
1863-1867

THE
POLITICS
OF
RECONSTRUCTION
1863-1867

DAVID DONALD

HARVARD UNIVERSITY PRESS
Cambridge, Massachusetts
London, England
1984

For BRUCE
who liked to work the calculating machine

Originally published in 1965 by Louisiana State
University Press

The Walter Lynwood Fleming Lectures
in Southern History, delivered at
Louisiana State University, April 1965

Library of Congress Cataloging in Publication Data

Donald, David Herbert, 1920–
    The politics of Reconstruction, 1863–1867.

    Reprint. Originally published: Baton Rouge:
Louisiana State University Press, 1965.   (The Walter
Lynwood Fleming lectures in southern history.)   With new
pref.
    Includes bibliographical references.
    1. Reconstruction.   2. United States—Politics and
government—1865–1869.   3. Republican Party   (U.S.:
1854–   ) —History—19th century.   I. Title.
II. Series: Walter Lynwood Fleming lectures in southern
history.
E668.D67   1984   973.81   83–22778
ISBN 0–674–68953–4

PREFACE, 1983

THIS BOOK WAS WRITTEN WHILE I WAS PREPARING *Charles Sumner and the Rights of Man*,[1] and it reflects some of the dissatisfaction I felt at that time with the state of Reconstruction historiography. After the very promising beginnings heralded in Howard K. Beale's 1940 article, "On Rewriting Reconstruction History,"[2] the Revisionist movement had lost most of its momentum by the 1960s, when many of the ablest historians of the period were involved in the much-publicized Civil War centennial observances. As I tried to understand Sumner's course during the postwar years, I found that there was in the secondary literature no reliable guide even to the proceedings of Congress during the Reconstruction era. Consequently I forced myself to read through, and to analyze, the thousands of pages of the *Congressional Globe* that recorded the interminable debates in the House of Representatives and the Senate during the 1860s and 1870s. *The Politics of Reconstruction* is a product of that research.

During the two decades since this little book was first published there have been many significant additions to the literature on Reconstruction, and I am happy to report that some of the lacunae noted in the preface to the original edition have now been filled. There are now a number of excellent studies of Reconstruction in individual states: George H. Thompson's *Arkansas and Reconstruction*;[3] Jerrell H. Shofner's *Nor Is It Over Yet*,[4] on Florida; Alan Conway's *The Reconstruction of Georgia*;[5] Elizabeth S. Nathans's *Losing the Peace*,[6] also on Georgia; Joe G. Taylor's *Louisiana Reconstructed*;[7] Jean H. Baker's *The Politics of Continuity*,[8] on Maryland; William C. Harris's *Presidential Reconstruction in Mississippi*[9] and his *The Day of the Carpetbagger*,[10] also on Mississippi. Vernon L. Wharton's monograph on Negroes in Mississippi is now flanked by Peter Kolchin's *First Freedom*,[11] on Alabama; Joe M. Richardson's *The Negro in the Reconstruction of Florida*;[12] and Joel Williamson's *After Slavery: The Negro in South Carolina during Reconstruction*.[13] There is still no definitive biography of Andrew Johnson, but William S. McFeely's *Grant*[14] authoritatively fills another gap that I lamented. I take great pride in noting that many of the recent studies of Reconstruction were originally doctoral dissertations that I directed.

Some of the arguments advanced in *The Politics of Reconstruction* have since been tested and refined by other historians. There has been general acceptance of my contention that the term "Radical Reconstruction" is a misnomer, since the major legislation of the postwar period was shaped by both Moderate and Radical Republicans, with occasional assistance from Conservative Republicans and even Democrats. Larry G. Kincaid has pointed out "the absurdity" of attributing such measures as the two Civil Rights Acts of the Reconstruction era, the Thirteenth, Fourteenth, and Fifteenth Amendments, the Military Reconstruction Acts, and the Enforcement Acts "to the quasi-conspiratorial activities of a relative handful of politicians—the radical Republicans."[15] Michael Les Benedict has also stressed the fundamentally conservative nature of Radical Reconstruction.[16] William Gillette demonstrated that the Fifteenth Amendment, once considered a high point of Radicalism, was, in fact, the result of a compromise between Republican factions and that its main features were "framed, championed, and secured by generally Republican moderates."[17]

The appeal I made for serious study of congressional proceedings and for careful analysis of factionalism within the dominant Republican party during the Civil War and Reconstruction years has also been heeded. Shortly after the appearance of *The Politics of Reconstruction*, Edward Gambill published his valuable essay, "Who Were the Senate Radicals?"[18] which used scaling techniques for delineating Republican factions. In a series of articles published between 1966 and 1970, and in a more recent book summarizing his findings,[19] Glenn M. Linden presented a quantitative analysis of numerous roll-call votes in Congress, especially those dealing with economic issues. Michael Les Benedict's comprehensive and impressive *A Compromise of Principle*[20] offered an even fuller study of the nature and consequences of Republican factionalism. In several articles and in a recent authoritative synthesis, *The Earnest Men: Republicans of the Civil War Senate*,[21] Allan G. Bogue has applied highly advanced quantitative techniques to this problem, and his essay, "Historians and Radical Republicans: A Meaning for Today,"[22] puts the whole issue into a larger perspective.

Since these studies differ in focus, in methodology, and in the time span they cover, it is not surprising that they also disagree somewhat in conclusions or that their several lists of members of Republican factions are not identical to those that I offered. What is surprising is the degree of consensus that emerges from these varied approaches. Thanks to them it is now possible to identify, with reasonable accuracy, most congressmen as belonging to one of the Republican factions.

We have not, I fear, achieved equal agreement on the origins of Republican factionalism. Allan Bogue has discovered rather more of a connection between Radicalism and economic policies favoring rapid expansion of industrial capitalism than have most other scholars. William R. Brock's view that Radical and Moderate Republicans came from different geographical backgrounds has found some support in recent writings. My own thesis, that a congressman's Radicalism varied with the degree of security he felt about his chances of being reelected, has not received adequate systematic testing. Professor Bogue believes that it does not hold for members of the Senate during the Civil War years; but I never claimed that it did, since senators, who were elected for long terms in office and were at that time indirectly chosen, by state legislatures, were relatively insulated from constituency pressures.

While this outpouring of books and articles is in some ways all that I could have hoped for when I called for further study of the politics of Reconstruction, it has in a certain sense been also a little disappointing. The extraordinary amount of time, energy, and methodological sophistication required to make systematic studies of congressional roll calls has to some degree made this sort of analysis an end in itself, and at times scholars seem to have forgotten that Guttman scalograms and voting-bloc clusters are important only if they help to understand how the political system worked. It might be useful to remember that, ideally, if a historian could find a single, perfectly focused roll-call vote, it would tell him as much about party factionalism as a computer analysis of many hundreds of largely repetitious votes.

Because of the attention given to these technical method-ological matters, the larger appeal I made in *The Politics of Reconstruction* has been somewhat overlooked. That can best be called an advocacy of "situational analysis"—the examina-tion of how, in any particular historical context, the options available to a politician are limited because of the position he occupies, because of his relationship to his peers within the governmental structure, and because of his ultimate need for endorsement by a majority of whatever electorate he repre-sents. Doubtless I urged this behavioristic approach with too great stridency. But I do think that Lincoln, Johnson, and the members of Congress were acutely aware that only a few courses were politically possible for them and that they acted within those felt constraints. If, like them, we can recognize the limitations embedded in their political situation, we can better understand both what they did and what they dared not try to do during the fateful Reconstruction years.

NOTES

1. *Charles Sumner and the Rights of Man* (New York: Alfred A. Knopf, 1970).

2. *American Historical Review*, 45 (1940):807–827.

3. *Arkansas and Reconstruction: The Influence of Geography, Economics, and Personality* (Port Washington, N.Y.: Kennikat Press, 1976).

4. *Nor Is It Over Yet: Florida in the Era of Reconstruction, 1863–1877* (Gainesville: University Presses of Florida, 1974).

5. *The Reconstruction of Georgia* (Minneapolis: University of Minnesota Press, 1966).

6. *Losing the Peace: Georgia Republicans and Reconstruction, 1865–1871* (Baton Rouge: Louisiana State University Press, 1968).

7. *Louisiana Reconstructed, 1863–1877* (Baton Rouge: Louisiana State Uni-versity Press, 1974).

8. *The Politics of Continuity: Maryland Political Parties from 1858 to 1870* (Baltimore: The John Hopkins University Press, 1973).

9. *Presidential Reconstruction in Mississippi* (Baton Rouge: Louisiana State University Press, 1967).

10. *The Day of the Carpetbagger: Republican Reconstruction in Mississippi* (Baton Rouge: Louisiana State University Press, 1978).

11. *First Freedom: The Responses of Alabama's Blacks to Emancipation and Reconstruction* (Westport, Conn.: Greenwood Press, 1972).

12. *The Negro in the Reconstruction of Florida, 1865–1877* (Tallahassee: Florida State University Press, 1965).

13. *After Slavery: The Negro in South Carolina during Reconstruction, 1861–1877* (Chapel Hill: University of North Carolina Press, 1965).

14. *Grant: A Biography* (New York: W. W. Norton and Co., 1981).

15. "Victims of Circumstance: An Interpretation of Changing Attitudes toward Republican Policy Makers and Reconstruction," *Journal of American History*, 57 (1970):48–66, especially p. 63.

16. "Preserving the Constitution: The Conservative Basis of Radical Reconstruction," *Journal of American History*, 61 (1974):65–90.

17. *The Right to Vote: Politics and the Passage of the Fifteenth Amendment* (Baltimore: The Johns Hopkins Press, 1965), especially p. 165.

18. *Civil War History*, 11 (1965):237–244.

19. " 'Radicals' and Economic Policies: The Senate, 1861–1873," *Journal of Southern History*, 32 (1966):188–199; " 'Radicals' and Economic Policies: The House of Representatives, 1861–1873," *Civil War History*, 13 (1967):51–65; " 'Radical' Political and Economic Polices: The Senate, 1873–1877," *Civil War History*, 14 (1968):240–249; "A Note on Negro Suffrage and Republican Politics," *Journal of Southern History*, 36 (1970):411–420; *Politics or Principle: Congressional Voting on the Civil War Amendments and Pro-Negro Measures, 1838–1869* (Seattle: University of Washington Press, 1976).

20. *A Compromise of Principle: Congressional Republicans and Reconstruction, 1863–1869* (New York: W. W. Norton and Co., 1974).

21. "Party and Bloc in the United States Senate: 1861–1863," *Civil War History*, 13 (1967):221–241; "The Radical Voting Dimension in the U.S. Senate during the Civil War," *Journal of Interdisciplinary History*, 3 (1967):449–474; "Some Dimensions of Power in the Thirty-Seventh Senate," in *The Dimensions of Quantitative Research in History*, ed. William O. Aydelotte et al. (Princeton: Princeton University Press, 1972), pp. 285–318; *The Earnest Men: Republicans of the Civil War Senate* (Ithaca: Cornell University Press, 1981).

22. *Journal of American History*, 70 (1983):7–34.

Preface to the First Edition

THOUGH 1965 IS THE APPROPRIATE YEAR, THERE HAS AS YET been no proposal for Congress to establish a National Reconstruction Centennial Commission. Unlike the events, great and small, of the Civil War, which we have recently celebrated, the 1866 New Orleans massacre is not likely to be re-enacted, and nobody has urged a full-dress restaging of the impeachment trial of President Andrew Johnson—even though, with a namesake in the White House, there is an obvious candidate for the leading role. The Reconstruction drama, it is clear, fails to fascinate the popular mind. To most Americans these postwar years seem a dark, unpleasant interlude of failure: failure of Southern whites to restore a social order which they cherished; failure of Negroes to secure basic civil rights; failure of the North to impose its values on the conquered section.

Yet, as the centennial approaches, there has been something of a revival of scholarly interest in Reconstruction. Kenneth M. Stampp's *The Era of Reconstruction, 1865–1877* is a judicious and lucid general reappraisal of the postwar years, and John Hope Franklin's *Reconstruction after the Civil War* gives deserved attention to the accomplishments of Southern Negroes. Eric L. McKitrick's *Andrew Johnson and Reconstruction,* LaWanda and John H. Cox's *Politics, Principle and Prejudice,* and William R. Brock's *An American Crisis* have, taken together, required a complete reinterpretation of Andrew Johnson's presidency. Several carefully researched and well-written biographies, such as Hans L. Trefousse's studies of Benjamin F. Butler and Benjamin F. Wade, Mrs. Fawn M. Brodie's life of Thaddeus Stevens, and the full-length portrait of Edwin M. Stanton by Benjamin P. Thomas and Harold M. Hyman, give clearer and more favorable accounts of the Republicans who fought against Johnson. Howard J. Graham, Joseph B. James, Jacobus ten Broek, and Alexander M. Bickel have published important revisionist work on the Fourteenth Amendment. Standard interpretations of the economic issues during Reconstruction have had to be revised in light of Robert P. Sharkey's *Money, Class and Party* and of Irwin F. Unger's *The Greenback Era,* and Ari A. Hoogenboom's *Outlawing the Spoils* requires us to give a new and more friendly look at the administrative history of the period. C. Vann Woodward's *Reunion and Reaction* has compelled us to take an entirely different view of the compromises which ended congressional Reconstruction.

There are still, however, far too many gaps in the record. Except for works on Tennessee, by T. B. Alexander, and on

Texas, by W. C. Nunn, no full-scale study of the postwar era in any Southern state has been published in the last twenty years, and the monographs written under the supervision of William A. Dunning half a century ago remain the standard accounts. There are no good books on the politics of any Northern state during Reconstruction. Despite the obvious importance of the Negro in the Reconstruction story, Vernon L. Wharton's monograph on *The Negro in Mississippi, 1865–1890*, published in 1947, still stands alone in the field. A study of the Federal Army in the postwar South is badly wanted, as is a major work on the constitutional issues of the whole period. Andrew Johnson still lacks a good biographer, and there is no perceptive account of Grant's presidency.

Useful as research along these and many other lines would be, even more valuable would be a fresh, general approach to the entire Reconstruction era. The excellent and invaluable studies now being published are more successful in refuting the old stereotypes about "Black Reconstruction" than in presenting that sweeping new interpretation for which Howard K. Beale called in 1940. We know today a great deal about what did not happen during Reconstruction, but we have not developed a new pattern for the period as a whole. At this point, however, the rewriting of Reconstruction history appears to have become curiously stalled.

In part this situation derives from the virtual exhaustion of the sources conventionally used by historians—public documents, newspapers, manuscripts. To be sure, the Coxes discovered a significant new source in the papers of S. L. M. Barlow, but most of the other important recent books on the period are based upon a reworking of documents long available. In his study of Andrew Johnson, Professor McKitrick does not "claim to have exploited materials which were not familiar to Howard Beale and George Milton back in 1930, or to others a generation before them," and Dr.

Brock dispenses with a bibliography for *An American Crisis,* noting, "This book makes no claim to open up new sources for Reconstruction history. . . ." There is no reason to think that other students of the period are going to be more successful in turning up new and revealing caches of manuscripts on the period.

In part, too, the present inconclusive state of Reconstruction historiography can be attributed to the fact that so much of it is biographical. It would be unfitting for me to belittle the art of biography, but it should be remembered that years of intensive research devoted to the life of one man sometimes causes the biographer to identify with his subject, and, understanding all, to forgive all. (Sometimes, of course, the reverse pattern occurs, and the biographer writes with passion to demolish his subject.) Necessarily the biographer is concerned with establishing the motives of his hero and of determining whether he is sincere, consistent, and loyal. But it does not greatly help us in reconstructing the Reconstruction era to learn that Benjamin F. Butler loved his wife and Charles Sumner hated his.

To some extent the deadlock in the writing of Reconstruction history is related to the fact that the central issues of the period, such as the role of the Negro in American society and the relative power of federal and state governments, are still very much with us. A generation ago a number of young historians, many of them Southerners, were attracted to study of the Reconstruction period because this seemed the best way of promoting the cause of civil rights, but to today's more engaged students writing monographs on the postwar years seems pallid when compared to participating in sit-ins or voter registration drives in the South. At the same time, historians who are less active in the civil rights crusade have understandably been wary of pursuing researches which might be misused to promote present-day bigotry or racial strife. They realize that an objective study of the freedmen at the end of the war will be used by today's racists to "prove" the Negroes' congenital inferiority; they know that exposure of selfish or neurotic motives on the part of Republican leaders will be distorted into a criticism of the causes which those leaders advocated; they fear that to reveal the part played by expediency and egotism in the adoption of Reconstruction legislation may seem to argue that the laws themselves were unnecessary or undesirable.

Finally, the present unpromising state of Reconstruction history reflects boredom with the questions students of the period have conventionally asked: Would it have been better to follow Lincoln's generous program toward the conquered whites than to insist upon harsher, Radical terms? Were the Radical Republicans right in demanding the ballot for the freedmen, instead of pushing for a division of Southern plantations among the Negroes? Were the "carpetbag" regimes set up in the South more corrupt than the contemporary governments in most Northern cities? Did the considerable accomplishments of these Radical Southern governments in the field of education and social welfare compensate for their undoubted inefficiency and venality? To such questions, involving value judgments, there can be no final answers, and it is hard to see how further research can be of much help in settling them.

The present little book is intended to suggest an approach which may bypass these roadblocks which have done so much to retard the rewriting of Reconstruction history. It consists of three exercises in applying techniques more frequently used in the behavioral sciences to the history of the Republican party during the years from 1863 to 1867, years during which this organization controlled the national government and set forth the conditions on which reunion could occur. In so brief a book I have necessarily had to omit much, and doubtless I have made errors of facts and of inference. But if the methods here used, and the conclusions here suggested, help any student see the fascinating complexities of the Reconstruction era which are yet to be explored my purpose will have been amply served.

These essays were originally presented as the Walter Lynwood Fleming lectures in Southern history at Louisiana State University on April 12 and 13, 1965. They are here published in substantially the same form in which they were delivered.

DAVID DONALD

The Johns Hopkins University
April, 1965

ACKNOWLEDGMENTS

I AM DEEPLY GRATEFUL TO THE MEMBERS OF THE HISTORY department at Louisiana State University, and particularly to the chairman, Professor John L. Loos, for inviting me to deliver the Walter Lynwood Fleming lectures in Southern history, and this book owes much to the kindly encouragement they gave me during my visit to Baton Rouge. To Professor T. Harry Williams my debt is a very special one, not alone for the perceptive reading which he gave the entire manuscript but for the critical stimulation which his own distinguished writings have afforded me over many years.

The first two chapters of this book, in preliminary form,

were presented to both the history and the political science seminars at the Johns Hopkins University, and I have greatly profited from the criticism of my colleagues. To Professors Alfred D. Chandler, Jr., Stephen E. Ambrose, Thomas I. Cook, and Francis E. Rourke I am especially grateful for stimulating suggestions, and Professor Robert L. Peabody's close reading of the manuscript has saved me from countless blunders. Mr. Sydney Nathans helped me see some of my stylistic weaknesses.

Taking time from his own researches on the Radical Republicans, Professor Hans L. Trefousse, of Brooklyn College, read proofs of the entire book, and his thorough knowledge of the period has been of invaluable assistance.

The Director of the Louisiana State University Press, Mr. Richard L. Wentworth, has taken a special and kindly interest in this book, and Mrs. Elizabeth Brown, of the Johns Hopkins Press, proved to be an ideal copy editor.

Thanks to a fellowship from the John Simon Guggenheim Memorial Foundation, I was able to complete this book without being under pressure from classroom duties.

My heaviest debt is to my wife, Aïda DiPace Donald, who not only shared with me her own expertise in the Civil War–Reconstruction era but who read the manuscript, the galley proofs, and the page proofs with searching care. Convention requires me to say that I alone am responsible for any errors that remain, but truth obliges me to add that she deserves the credit for whatever degree of accuracy and clarity the book may claim.   D.D.

CONTENTS

FIGURES

TABLES

CHAPTER

I

THE
MECHANICS OF
MODERATION

NOWHERE HAVE HISTORIANS OF RECONSTRUCTION REACHED a more complete stalemate than in their interpretations of the Republican party. Everybody recognizes the enormous importance of the party. Except for the three years of Andrew Johnson's defection to the Democrats, the Republicans controlled the presidency from the beginning of the Civil War through what we have come to call the restoration of "home rule" in the South sixteen years later. In all but the last two years of this period, both houses of Congress were solidly under Republican control. Every major step in the political rebuilding of the Union was the work of the Republican party: Lincoln's 10 per cent plan; the Wade-Davis bill; the Freedmen's Bureau bill; the Civil Rights Act; the Fourteenth Amendment; the 1867 Reconstruction Act, with its later supplements; and the Fifteenth Amendment. On the national

1

scene the history of Reconstruction is substantially the history of the Republican party.

Only a few years ago we knew exactly how to narrate this history. Following T. Harry Williams, J. G. Randall, and William B. Hesseltine on the Civil War years and Howard K. Beale and George Fort Milton on the Reconstruction period, we agreed that the Republican party was, from the beginning, split into rival factions. On the one hand were the Moderates (or Conservatives), who rallied around Abraham Lincoln and later Andrew Johnson; on the other were the Radicals, led by such vindictives as Charles Sumner, Thaddeus Stevens, and Benjamin F. Wade.

The Moderates, everybody knew, had sought to prevent the outbreak of the Civil War and, once it began, tried to keep it, as Lincoln said, from degenerating "into a violent and remorseless revolutionary struggle." A farseeing statesman, Lincoln wanted to end the war without rankling bitterness. He entreated the Northerners to exhibit malice toward none and charity for all; Southerners he begged to repent themselves of rebellion and return to the Union; Negroes he urged to be content with their new-found freedom, even perhaps with a gradual emancipation stretching on to 1900. Painlessly readmitting the reconstructed rebel states as soon as they showed signs of loyalty, he would have bound up the nation's wounds, so that Americans could live in peace. Andrew Johnson, after a momentary aberration, continued this Lincolnian program into the postwar years.

Against these forces of moderation were pitted the Radicals, or Jacobins, whose main characteristics, according to J. G. Randall, were "antislavery zeal as a political instrument, moralizing unction, rebel-baiting intolerance and hunger for power." "Aggressive, vindictive, and narrowly sectional," they had welcomed the outbreak of the war, and they feared it might end before they could free the slaves and break up the estates of the Southern planters. Their motives, some standard historians admitted, were partly humanitarian if misguided, but their chief purpose was to humiliate the Southern whites and to guarantee continued dominance of the Republican party, so as to favor the big business interests which they represented. High tariffs, enormous railroad land grants, exploitation of the public domain through a homestead system, a national banking system which discriminated against the agrarian South and West, and "sound" money which favored the creditor classes were the instruments through which they guaranteed business control of the nation's economic life. Using the Negro as a pawn in their game, these unsavory Radicals conspired against Lincoln, humiliated and hamstrung Johnson, and, under the Reconstruction Act of 1867, imposed their will on the prostrate South. Only the political incapacity of the freedmen, the growing resentment of the Southern whites, and the aroused sense of injustice in the North brought, by 1877, an end to their carnival of exploitation and extravagance.

I

In the last decade historians have been busily at work reshading and redrawing portions of this panorama, and, as a result of their efforts, it is now hard even to determine the lines of battle. Once considered the sole repository of virtue, the Moderate Republicans have recently been having a hard time of it. After exposing Abraham Lincoln's extraconstitutional measures which, he claimed, largely subverted the original structure of our federal system, Professor Hesseltine argued that the Civil War President had not one but many conflicting policies on Reconstruction. Mr. McKitrick has sketched Andrew Johnson as a blundering outsider, while LaWanda and John H. Cox paint him as a provincial Negrophobe.

On the other hand, recent biographers of Wade, Butler, Stevens, and Stanton stress the sincerity of the Radicals' concern for the Negro. Simultaneously Robert P. Sharkey, Irwin F. Unger, and Stanley Coben have noted the diversity of the Radicals' views on economic issues and have demolished the idea that they represented a monolithic business community. In an unpublished dissertation, Dr. Glenn M. Linden has analyzed congressional voting patterns on 160 economic issues and concludes: ". . . 'Radicalism' in Congress from 1861 to 1873 did not include an identifiable stand on economic measures."

It has even become hard to identify a distinctively Radical position on such questions as slavery, confiscation of Confederate property, Negro voting, and the readmission of Southern states. To illustrate the problem one has only to turn to the two principal and antagonistic spokesmen of Massachusetts during this period. There can be no doubt that Senator Charles Sumner was a Radical and that Charles Francis Adams, Lincoln's minister to Great Britain, was a self-styled Conservative, and to their ideological differences personal and political rivalries lent a special bitterness.

But when war came, both men at once recognized its revolutionary possibilities. Sumner went to the White House and jubilantly informed Lincoln that "under the war power the right had come to him to emancipate the slaves." At about the same time Adams concluded: "We cannot afford to go over this ground more than once. The slave question must be settled this time once for all."

As the war dragged drearily along, Sumner incessantly nagged the President to act against slavery, partly to weaken the Confederacy at home, partly to strengthen the Union abroad. "Slavery . . . our Catiline, being to this war everything,—inspiration, motive-power, end and aim, be-all and end-all," must be abolished, he announced. In faraway

London, Adams disapproved of the revolutionary tone of Sumner's speech, but he wrote home privately—no doubt intending that his sentiments should be passed along to the President—that there was an "absolute necessity" for Lincoln to influence European opinion by declaring "the truth—which is that the slave question must be settled" before the United States could consider any peace offer.

When Lincoln continued to hesitate, Sumner began to worry that peace might come too soon. "We are too victorious," he lamented; "I fear more from our victories than from our defeats. . . . There must be more delay and more suffering, —yet another 'plague' before all will agree to 'let my people go': and the war cannot, must not, end till then." This undoubtedly Radical sentiment had its counterpart in Adams' diary entry made after Gettysburg: "A little more of success on our part would complete the business. It may be however that the proper time has not yet arrived. Slavery though shaken is not utterly overthrown. Perhaps it is part of the Divine dispensation that the hearts of these people remain hardened until the end of emancipation be fully accomplished."

Long before the end of the war Sumner was moving to revolutionize the South by guaranteeing education, homesteads, civil rights, and the franchise to the Negroes, pledging that "for a while the freedman will take the place of the master, verifying the saying that the last shall be first and the first shall be last." The Conservative Adams shared Sumner's zeal for reorganizing the conquered section. "We must not settle with them until their social system has assumed a very different aspect," the Minister wrote his son. "Their population is naturally a purely agricultural one. It must be brought to have a stake in the soil it cultivates. . . . The mass are now nearly barbarous whilst the few are passionate and violent. I think they have already had something of a severe lesson.

But it will not avail, unless they are made to cease to be
masters over their fellow creatures."

Between Sumner and Adams there were, of course, differences, and important ones, in method and even more in
temperament, but it is useful to remember that Adams for-
bade his friends to present him as a candidate against Sumner
in the Massachusetts senatorial elections of 1863 and 1869.
Cordially disliking Sumner and vigorously reprobating his
harsh tone and unabashed pedantry, Adams recognized that
he and his rival shared most major political objectives.

Lest it be said that Sumner and Adams were two excep-
tional cases, it is well to note that their sentiments on major
wartime issues were shared by Moderate and Radical Republicans from other parts of the country. It is hard to find
important Civil War issues which aligned congressional
Radicals against the President and the Moderates. Naturally
Republican legislators often disagreed over the precise form
or specific provisions of a bill, but it is not easy to discover
either in the debates or in the preliminary roll calls any clear
factional alignments. On the other hand the final votes on
virtually all measures relating to the prosecution of the war,
slavery, and the reorganization of the South showed an
amazing Republican unanimity. The First Confiscation Act
of 1861, often taken as the opening gun in the Radicals' war
upon the South, passed the Senate without a division; in the
House it received the support of 59 Republicans and was
opposed by only 9;[1] and it was signed by the President. The
more stringent Second Confiscation Act of 1862 was backed
by 82 Republicans in the House and was opposed by only
5, 4 of whom came from the Border States; in the Senate 27

---

[1] Most of these nine were from the Border States and were not genuine Republicans. Edward McPherson's *The Political History of the United States
of America, during the Great Rebellion* (3d ed.; Washington, 1876), from
which all the figures in this paragraph are taken, groups "Unionists" of
various descriptions together with regular Republicans.

Republicans voted for it, and only 4, including 2 from the Border States, opposed; and, after slight modification, it too was approved by Lincoln. In December, 1862, 76 Republican Congressmen voted to endorse Lincoln's Emancipation Proclamation, and only 7, mostly again from the Border States, opposed. No Republican in either House or Senate opposed the Thirteenth Amendment, to end slavery in the land, when it came to a vote in 1864, and when it came before Congress again in January, 1865, once more every voting Republican in the House supported it. In this last vote Lincoln showed his solidarity with his party by quietly maneuvering to secure one or two necessary Democratic votes, and then he took the unprecedented, and unnecessary, step of signing the joint resolution submitting the amendment to the states for ratification.

This substantial unanimity among Republicans of all factions during the Civil War has been statistically documented by Dr. Linden, in his careful tabulation of congressional ballots on all major measures dealing with the Confederacy and the freedmen. He has found only two Republican Senators, Edgar Cowan of Pennsylvania and Waitman T. Willey of West Virginia, and only five Representatives, three of them from the Border States, who failed to support at least half of all so-called "Radical" measures between 1861 and 1865.

Not even the end of the war, the death of Lincoln, and the accession of Andrew Johnson to the presidency broke the pattern of Republican solidarity in Congress. Thaddeus Stevens' motion, in February, 1866, to deny representation to the rebel states until both houses of Congress should give consent was supported by 109 Republican Representatives and opposed by only 8, largely from the Border States; in the Senate, 29 Republicans endorsed the measure and only 8 voted against it. Opposition to the Freedmen's Bureau bill

of 1866 included no Republican Senators and only one
Republican Representative. In the same year 33 Republican
Senators voted for the Civil Rights bill, while only 3 opposed; 111 Republican Representatives supported the
measure, and only 6 opposed. In both houses there were but
3 Republicans who joined the Democrats in voting against
final passage of the Fourteenth Amendment.

Even after Johnson broke with his party and tried desperately to lure Moderates into following his course, the Republicans in Congress continued to present an almost unbroken
front. Only one Republican Senator and nine Republican
Representatives voted in 1867 against extending the suffrage
to Negroes in the District of Columbia. Only five Republican
Representatives voted against final passage of the Reconstruction bill of 1867; no Republican Senator opposed. Only four
Republican Representatives and two Republican Senators
fought the passage of the Tenure of Office Act. Again Dr.
Linden's tabulations are useful in reinforcing this point, for
he finds during these postwar years only four Republican
Senators and only eight Republican Representatives who
failed to support allegedly "Radical" legislation at least 50
per cent of the time.

II

The historian of the Republican party, which played such
a vital role in shaping the pattern of Reconstruction, is thus
faced with a baffling problem. We know, as did every acute
observer at the time and as has every perceptive historian
since, that there were indeed rival Radical and Moderate
factions among the Republicans, and we know that their
rivalry was of central importance to the Reconstruction story.
At the same time we are unable clearly to identify the membership of either Moderate or Radical factions or to attribute to either distinctive views on the conduct of the war, on

the rehabilitation of the South, or on general economic policies.

This problem of defining the membership and policies of the Republican factions, it should be observed at the outset, is not to be solved by laudation of either Moderate or Radical leaders. To declare that Moderates like Johnson and Lincoln were statesmanlike and magnanimous while Radicals were characterized by partisanship, vindictiveness, and false humanitarianism reveals the social objectives which a historian believes desirable but tells us little about the composition or ideology of the conflicting groups. On the other hand, it is equally unilluminating to argue that Radicals were men of deeper devotion to human rights and of purer commitment to the principles of equality than were their Conservative counterparts. It would be a shrewd Solomon who could judge between the moral purity of a Charles Sumner and a Charles Francis Adams. Nor would it be easy to prove that the sinuous course of Radical Benjamin F. Butler was more devious than that of Conservative Nathaniel P. Banks. Name-calling, in short, is not historical analysis, and the historian must be specially wary of that oldest of fallacies, that the advocates of good causes have good motives.

One of the few historians who have thoughtfully confronted this central problem of Reconstruction historiography is T. Harry Williams, who in a revision of his earlier interpretation of Republican factionalism has showed that the Radicals differed on economic goals, that they shared many objectives with the Moderates, and that they often cooperated with Lincoln. At the same time, Professor Williams properly maintains that real differences did exist among Republicans, and he suggests that Radicals may be distinguished by their "doctrinaire and dogmatic" spirit and by their failure to advocate "pragmatic or empiric" approaches to Reconstruction.

These distinctions, Professor Williams would be the first
to admit, are hard to document. It was, after all, an age
when everybody in every party was uttering a good deal of
doctrine and dogma. Doubtless Sumner's pronouncement
that nothing in favor of human rights could be contrary to
the Constitution was doctrinaire—but so was Democratic
Senator Reverdy Johnson's literal-minded insistence upon
legal technicalities when the nation's very existence was at
stake. Thaddeus Stevens' proposal to confiscate and divide
up Southern plantations was revolutionary, to be sure, but
what else can we call Conservative Thurlow Weed's plan to
have the entire South, "whether it be farms, plantations, vil-
lages or cities, . . . partitioned equitably . . . among the
officers and soldiers by whom it shall have been conquered"?
Nor is it easy to follow Professor Williams' suggestion that
Radicals exhibited a distinctive personality type. The difficulty here is that the historian of Reconstruction knows, and
can know, so little about any of the Radicals except a handful
of familiar leaders. It is not enough to generalize about
Sumner, Stevens, Wade, and Chandler; the analysis must
include numerous Radical Republican Congressmen like
James M. Ashley and Samuel Shellabarger, John M. Broomall
and Portus Baxter, about whom the historian can find almost
no biographical data that are psychologically revealing.

Aside from Professor Williams, the only historian seriously
to tackle the problem of Republican factionalism in the
light of recent scholarship is the English scholar, W. R.
Brock, who has tried to separate Radicals from Moderates
on the basis of their vote on a key, preliminary test of the
Reconstruction Act of 1867. Though a single roll-call analysis
is not, as Dr. Brock admits, entirely adequate for precise
definition, the one vote which he selected was indeed crucial,
and the line he traces between Republican factions is the
most objective yet constructed. But after this auspicious be-

ginning, Dr. Brock starts on a false trail. The congressional districts whose Representatives voted for the Radical Reconstruction proposal in 1867, he finds, were chiefly rural areas, heavily concentrated in the recently settled Middle and Far West, and he postulates, therefore, that Radicalism may have been the result of "a hitherto unsuspected influence of the frontier upon American history." Perhaps this last suggestion was not intended very seriously, but it is startling to think of Charles Sumner, Wendell Phillips, Benjamin F. Butler, and Thaddeus Stevens as authentic voices of the American frontier. More important, Dr. Brock fails to recognize that most Republican districts in the 1860's were rural, since the larger cities were usually Democratic, and the overwhelmingly Radical vote of Pennsylvania Congressmen upsets the geographical pattern he has tried to trace.

III

Perhaps in searching for some occult bond that united men of differing backgrounds, ideas, and motives, the historian of Reconstruction has made his task unnecessarily complicated. Having for the initial purpose of convenience classified his Republicans as Radicals or Moderates, he tends to take his classifications too seriously; they become groups, and these groups in turn are personified and are expected to have a common life history or a common mind. In everyday life, of course, we are all aware that such personification is impossible. The members of a public group, whether it be a religious organization, a social club, an academic faculty, or a political party, come from various backgrounds, have differing amounts of money and prestige, and are impelled by many, and often mixed, motives. It would be well if we could similarly learn to live comfortably with the fact that Radical William Boyd Allison was the product of frontier Iowa and Radical John B. Alley was one of manufacturing

Massachusetts, that Radical Benjamin F. Butler was as flexible as Radical Sumner was doctrinaire, that Radical Thaddeus Stevens may have been moved by disinterested love of the oppressed and Radical Ashley by a desire for a lucrative federal office.

After recognizing these diversities, we might then profitably concentrate upon the one thing which historians can agree the members of each Republican faction had in common, namely, their voting record. In other words, what united Radical Republicans was not a special geographical origin, social status, psychological bent, or ideological preference, but the fact that they supported, and in Congress voted for, certain measures relating to the prosecution of the Civil War and the restoration of the South. And, in turn, what united the Moderates was their support of, and their voting for, other measures relating to the same subjects.

Since we have been unable to explain on the basis of ideology, social background, or motivation why some Republicans became Radicals while others were Moderates, perhaps it would be helpful to try a much simpler, more obvious approach. Let us assume as a working hypothesis that most politicians either wish to be re-elected to their present offices or aspire to higher ones. This assumption, it must be stressed, does not circuitously reintroduce the problem of motivations, for a politician may desire continuance in office for many reasons—personal, pecuniary, or altruistic. Nor should it be taken as an implicit value judgment, for to say that politicians want office is no more praise, nor condemnation, than to observe that bees seek nectar.

Pursuing this thesis, then let us look at the political facts which affected all Republicans of the Civil War and Reconstruction era. The most important of these was the very close political balance which existed between the two great national parties in virtually every presidential election from

1828 through 1892. The Whigs, and their successors, the Republicans, carried nine of these seventeen elections, but these victories did not reflect the existence of any anti-Democratic majority in the country as a whole. Rutherford B. Hayes in 1876 and Benjamin Harrison in 1888 received fewer votes than their Democratic rivals, and James A. Garfield in 1880 had a plurality of only 40,000. The two Whig presidential victories came in 1840 and 1848, when that party nominated ostensibly nonpartisan military heroes. The Republicans continued this tradition in Grant's two elections after the Civil War. Lincoln was first elected in 1860 with less than 40 per cent of the total national vote, and his sweeping success in 1864 can properly be evaluated only if we remember that the Southern Democrats had other things on their mind that year. In fact, so often were Whig-Republican presidential victories during this period attributable to disproportionate electoral arrangements, to division among their opponents, to disfranchisement of Southerners after the war, and to the charisma of their candidates that some scholars have called the Democrats in the mid-nineteenth century the party of the permanent majority.

Of as great importance, however, was the other elementary political fact that Democratic and Republican strength was not evenly distributed over the entire country, or even over an entire state. In Indiana, for example, Republicans cast only 44 per cent of the total vote in the first congressional district, but 62 per cent of the voters in the fifth district supported that party. Moreover, there was great stability in these local voting patterns. States often shifted from one party to another, but there were counties (which, it will be remembered, chose the state legislators, who still elected the United States Senators) and congressional districts which the Democrats invariably carried and others which the Republicans always won. Though Republican control of the presidency was in doubt every four years, a great many congressional seats were virtually the permanent property of that party. Indiana, for instance, flirted with both parties in presidential contests, going Republican in 1860, 1864, 1868, and 1876, but voting Democratic in 1856 and 1872. Despite these vacillations, twenty-eight of its ninety-two counties went Republican in all these elections, while twenty-eight others as consistently voted Democratic.

IV

These two elementary political facts are alone enough to explain the Moderate course toward the South adopted by every Republican President of the period, from Lincoln through Rutherford B. Hayes. During the Civil War, though Lincoln's political tasks were in a sense simplified by the secession of the South and the consequent failure of the Confederate states to vote in the 1862 and 1864 elections, the President was obliged to build a broad coalition if he sought successfully to prosecute the war and to win re-election for himself and his party.

On the two wings of the Republican party he knew he could count so long as he retained firm control of the party machinery. A state like Vermont, which gave him 75 per cent of its vote in 1860 and 76 per cent in 1864, was certainly not going to vote Democratic, no matter what he did. Abolitionists demanding a vindictive war upon the South were rampant in such states, but Lincoln knew he did not have to heed their advice. They might carp and grumble, but they could not back a Democrat, and even if they all stayed at home on election day, their states would still go Republican. In fact, these states were so safe that the President could gain from offending some of these antislavery stalwarts, even to the extent of allowing his abolitionist critics to drift off into the third-party movement for John C. Frémont in 1864. As

President Harry S. Truman proved in 1948, the elimination of either the left or right extremes of a party may strengthen its appeal to the far more numerous, and more strategically placed, doubtful voters in the middle. So Wendell Phillips' fierce denunciations of Lincoln in 1864 undoubtedly helped convince wavering voters of the President's essential moderation.

It was these doubtful voters in the Northern and Border States whom the President had to woo in order to build his coalition. Lincoln's narrow margin of victory in 1860 and the defeats suffered by his party in the congressional elections of 1862 were sharp reminders that the Republicans could not count upon majority support in the nation as a whole. Only by splitting the opposition could the President strengthen his party in the doubtful counties of those states on which the next presidential election would turn. Much of Lincoln's political activity during the war, then, was necessarily devoted to efforts to lure some Democrats into his own party and to widen the split between those who remained outside, the War Democrats, who generally supported his policies, and the Peace Democrats, who opposed them.

To attract Democratic or undecided voters repelled by the Republican label, he had his political organization rechristened the National Union party. At the same time he sought to seduce some of the leaders of the Democratic opposition. Regardless of competence, Democrats were given army commands, and a good many of them followed Butler and Grant in becoming converts to the Republican faith. He appointed a few influential Democrats, like Edwin M. Stanton, to high civil office, and flirted with others, as when he sent word that if Democratic Governor Horatio Seymour of New York cooperated he could even become President in 1864. As crowning evidence of nonpartisanship, Lincoln saw that his rechristened party named a Southerner and a War

Democrat for the second highest—and surely least powerful
—office in the land.

The need to win Democratic votes in the marginal states
clearly pointed to the policies Lincoln must follow. Regardless of his own personal wishes and regardless of much
grumbling among Republicans, he procrastinated in moving
against slavery. If the Border States were not to be lost, he
must talk of gradual, compensated emancipation; if the
Negrophobic Southern half of the Old Northwest was not to
be conceded to the Democrats, he had to couple freeing
of the slaves with projects of colonizing them abroad.

Of course Lincoln had to take some steps which offended
Democratic sensibilities, but the necessity of strengthening
his party nationally shaped the style in which he acted.
Clearly sectional or partisan legislation, such as that relating
to confiscation of Southern property, increased tariffs, or
the national banking system, he allowed to seem to be the
work of Congress alone. So successful was he that, though he
in fact signed all these measures into law, to this day nobody
ever thinks of talking about "Lincoln's tariff" or "Lincoln's
banking system." When finally compelled to conciliate antislavery opinion at home and abroad by proclaiming emancipation, he justified his action not by its desirability or
morality but on the nonpartisan grounds of military necessity.
All the while he was obliged to project the image of himself
as being above party and to urge his Democratic critics to
rise above mere partisanship to meet him on the "higher
level" of disinterested national statesmanship.

So imperative was this necessity for the President to
broaden the basis of his support if he wanted re-election that
Lincoln's stance became one of calculated ambiguity, so
uncertain that no group within his own party could fully
claim him or be entirely satisfied with him. To Radicals he
often appeared "an awful, woeful ass," "the 'Good natured

man' without any spinal column," while to Moderates he frequently seemed to be entirely "under the control of the Greeley's—Sumners and band of 'fanatics' of the North." Yet both groups ultimately voted for him in 1864, as did many Northern War Democrats.

To explain Lincoln's success, and to explain his policy, it is, thus, not necessary to resort to biography and it is not even relevant to speak of his quaint charm, his passion for funny stories, or his inspiring eloquence. A rather simple computer installed in the White House, fed the elementary statistical information about election returns and programed to solve the recurrent problem of winning re-election, would emerge with the same strategies and the same solutions.

V

During the Reconstruction years these same political facts even more insistently obliged any Republican in the White House to follow a Moderate, or even a Conservative, course. The end of the war meant that the former Confederate states would sooner or later have to be readmitted to the Union, electing Congressmen and voting for a presidential candidate in all probability by 1868. If their electoral votes were Democratic, as all except those from Tennessee and Virginia had been in the three presidential elections before the war, the Republican party could only look forward to a future of defeat.

There were only three possible ways to prevent this development. One would be through a stringent program of disfranchising ex-Confederates, so as to turn over the restored Southern governments to the loyalists of that region, who would vote Republican. One trouble with this plan was that there were simply not enough of these men in most Southern states. Secretary of the Treasury Hugh McCulloch tried hard to employ only loyalists as his customs officers and tax collectors in the South, but he reported that he was obliged to recruit ex-Confederates in order to get his department's work done. Moreover, the loyalists of the South were mostly not suited for political leadership. One of James A. Garfield's correspondents characterized them as "men of no capacity or character . . . filled with personal ambition or malice . . . an element as weak in heads and hearts as in numbers." Such words were harsh and not fair when applied in individual cases, but it was true that these Southern white opponents of the Confederacy were not a sound basis on which to build a Republican party in that region.

A second possibility would have been the enfranchising of the freedmen, who, together with the white Unionists, might have kept many Southern states Republican. But such a course seemed to cost the party the national election of 1868, for racial prejudice was strong in the North. Republicans themselves differed as to the desirability of Negro suffrage, and, if made a party test, it would assuredly drive away the Democrats who had hitherto hesitantly voted with the Republican party and at the same time would force the War Democratic faction back into the arms of the Peace Democracy.

There was left, then, the third and only politically viable course, that of entrusting Reconstruction to the same Southern whites who had fought for the Confederacy, imposing minimal checks upon the new governments which they established and hoping through generous treatment to secure their future political support.

Such simple political considerations are quite enough to account for the fact that Abraham Lincoln grew increasingly lenient toward the wayward Southerners as the war drew to an end. In 1861 he used troops to keep Maryland and Missouri in the Union, and in 1862 he established provisional governments in the conquered areas of the South under military auspices. But in 1863 he was willing to grant self-government to the subdued states if only 10 per cent of the 1860 voters swore to future loyalty, and by 1865 he was prepared, until his cabinet overruled him, to give quasi-recognition to the secessionist government of Virginia.

Even more striking is the way these identical political considerations necessarily shaped Andrew Johnson's course. Not temperamentally inclined to moderation, he had spent his whole political life prior to his presidency fighting the established Southern leadership which had carried his state and his section into secession and war. Refusing to follow his state, he had remained in Congress as a fierce opponent of the Confederacy and of the Peace Democrats of the North who sympathized with it, and he was sufficiently Radical to win a place on the Joint Committee on the Conduct of the War, headed by Benjamin F. Wade. After Tennessee was overrun by Federal troops in 1862, Johnson accepted Lincoln's appointment as provisional governor of that state and supervised its reconstruction, harshly disfranchising Confederate sympathizers, suppressing disaffected newspapers, and dealing out military justice to the foes of the Union. When assassination made him President, Radicals felt sure they now had an ally in the White House, and Wade, leading a congressional delegation to visit the new Chief Executive, rejoiced: "Johnson, we have faith in you. By the gods, there will be no trouble now in running the government."

"I am very much obliged to you gentlemen," Johnson replied, "and I can only say you can judge of my policy by the past. Everybody knows what that is. I hold this: Robbery is a crime; murder is a crime; *treason* is a crime; and *crime* must be punished. . . . Treason must be made infamous and traitors must be impoverished."

During the next few weeks, Radicals thronged about the new President, sure of a sympathetic hearing. Sumner, who had feared Lincoln's moderate policy augured "confusion and uncertainty in the future,—with hot controversy," now had long conversations with Johnson, who saw "the rights and necessities of the case" for Negro suffrage and declared "there is no difference between us." Convinced that Johnson was going to require Negro voting as a condition for read-mission to the Union, Chief Justice Salmon P. Chase made a special trip through the former Confederacy to smooth the way for Southern acceptance of this revolutionary idea, and he confidently predicted it would prove so successful that "the people will be as little willing to spare Andrew Johnson from their service as to spare Andrew Jackson." When doubters spoke up in the Republican caucus before Congress adjourned, Sumner and Wade "both insisted that the Presi-dent was in no danger, and declared, furthermore, that he was in favor of negro suffrage," and Sumner rejoiced that Congress was disbanding so that control of the Reconstruc-tion process would be in Johnson's safe hands.

Yet within twelve months of his inauguration, this same Andrew Johnson publicly denounced both Sumner and Stevens, respected spokesmen of the party which had elected him; vetoed both the Freedmen's Bureau bill and the Civil Rights bill, supported by virtually the entire Republican delegation in both houses of Congress; set up in every former Confederate state governments which were dominated by men who for four years had been fighting against the Union; pardoned thousands of former rebel leaders; announced that his restored Southern governments ought to receive repre-sentation in Congress; and declared that the problem of Reconstruction was over.

This remarkable transformation is not to be explained away by arguing that the President never really espoused Radicalism, that he merely listened to all points of view in silence and his interviewers went away confusing his ideas with their own words. Sumner, Wade, Chase, and Grant all independently testified that he favored a stern Reconstruction program, a program in accord with his own previous conduct as provisional governor of Tennessee. Nor can it be accounted for by claiming that beneath Johnson's change lay a deeper consistency, his firm and inflexible adherence to the letter of the Constitution. Doubtless Johnson did believe in the Constitution—as did most Americans—and doubtless he rationalized his actions to bring them, at least in his own mind, to conform with that document. But in fact his constitutionalism was flexible. In 1864 as wartime governor in Tennessee he had flouted the Constitution by imposing an extraordinary oath disqualifying not merely secessionist sympathizers but those loyalists who intended to vote for George B. McClellan. When challenged, he retorted: "Suppose you do violate law if by so doing you restore the law and the constitution, your conscience will approve your course, and all the people will say, amen!" Nor during the Reconstruction years did he hesitate, despite the total lack of any constitutional authority, to appoint provisional governors for the former Confederate states, to issue instructions for the establishment of new regimes there, and to impose on them basic conditions before they could be restored to the Union. Nor can we accept the explanation that Johnson, a poor white, was so flattered because Southern aristocrats now fawned on him that he pardoned them and permitted them to resume political control. Like every other Southern politician from the poorer classes, Johnson had attracted such attentions long before the war, and he had not been tempted by them. The fact that the President was a gentleman, courteous even to visitors who had once worn the Confederate uniform, is no evidence that social attentions turned his head.

Practical political considerations, rather than personal

motivations, can best account for the President's switch to moderation. If he and his party were to be successful in 1868, when the states of the former Confederacy would probably be back in the Union, he must not merely retain Lincoln's coalition of Radicals, Moderates, and War Democrats, but he must add a considerable vote from the South. His wartime experience in his own state had taught him that there were not enough capable white Unionists to insure control of the reorganized Southern governments. The political danger of enfranchising the Negro he understood, all the more fully because he largely shared the racist views of Northern Democrats and many Republicans. In 1863 he had bluntly told an audience in Negrophobic Indiana: "If, as the car of state moves along, the negroes get in the way, let them be crushed." He saw no alternative, therefore, to working with ex-Confederates.

Following this necessary course did not, however, mean that Johnson could count upon re-election. Too rapid restoration of the Southern states under the leadership of former Confederates would certainly cost him the support of many Radicals. At the same time, prompt readmission of the Southern states under ex-Confederates would so increase the Democratic prospects for victory in 1868 that many Northern Democrats, who had uneasily supported Lincoln's coalition government during the war, would drift back to their original party, if only in the expectation of loaves and fishes. Gloatingly S. L. M. Barlow, the editor of the influential Democratic New York *World* predicted that the return of Southern Representatives would give the Democrats "an absolute majority in both branches of Congress." He added that Johnson would be obliged to go along with that majority, for "he will then be under the control of our organization, or powerless outside of it."

Confronted with this problem, Johnson, far from showing

himself a blundering politician or a temperamental "outsider," proved himself a virtuoso of politics. He kept his policies so vague that virtually everybody could endorse them. Even when Congress reassembled in December, 1865, the hyperthyroid Radicals like Sumner and Stevens were unable to organize any opposition to the President. Johnson's annual message, which George Bancroft wrote in fluent, ambiguous style, suggested to some that the President considered his steps toward Reconstruction as tentative, to others that he would make no backward move. At the same time, the President made as few appointments or removals as possible, realizing that every new officeholder would tend to identify him with one of the conflicting elements in the coalition he was trying to build. His intervention in local elections, such as the gubernatorial contest in Connecticut, was, as LaWanda and John Cox have shown, a masterpiece of procrastination and ambiguity.

As a result of these tactics of silence, delay, and confusion, so similar to those which identical political circumstances compelled Lincoln to follow, Johnson during his first twelve months of office received more praise and general support than had his predecessor. By the fall of 1865 a few articulate Radicals were restive, but even Sumner, sure that the President was off on a desperately wrong course, could only advise his friends to wait so "that the President shall break with us and not we with him." Moderate Republicans were content, believing that soon the President, guided by William H. Seward and Gideon Welles, would cast off the Radicals and create a new party of the center. Simultaneously, the Northern Democrats claimed Johnson was one of their very own, "a Democrat, following Democratic principle." And in the South, as numerous letters in the Johnson manuscripts show, he was the most popular man in the country.

Had Andrew Johnson died in January, 1866, he would

have gone down in our history books as one of our most politically astute Presidents. Yet within a few months of that date he split the party which elected him, was repudiated by the Democratic party as well, and narrowly escaped removal from his high office. It would be as misleading to attribute Johnson's downfall to such personal traits as inflexibility of temper or intemperateness of language as it would be to suggest that his earlier success had been due to the absence of these traits. So long as he staved off any real action on the part of Congress or the Southern states, he could hide behind ambiguities of language and keep with him the conflicting elements of his coalition. But when positive action had to be taken, the President was forced into the open, and his coalition disintegrated.

The passage of the Freedmen's Bureau bill in February, 1866, forced Johnson's hand. He might have signed the bill, for both Senators Lyman Trumbull and William Pitt Fessenden, after long, separate conferences with the President, were convinced that he basically agreed with its principles, and such a course would have kept the Radical and Moderate Republicans together. It would, however, assuredly have alienated the War Democrats, who had spoken up vigorously in Congress against the bill, and they were an indispensable element in any coalition Johnson might attempt to form. He might have allowed the bill to become law without his signature, but these same Democrats warned publicly that "words amount to nothing unless verified by deeds." He might have followed Seward's advice and vetoed the bill on purely technical grounds, but this tricky course could well alienate both Radicals and Democrats.

There seemed, therefore, no possible course but to veto the measure, and the strong language with which Johnson rejected the bill, coupled with his harsh and intemperate harangue against Radical Republicans in an informal address on Washington's birthday shortly afterwards, suggests the bitterness in the President's heart as he felt forced to this decision. There is some reason to believe that his heartache was the greater because he had not originally intended to take a stand on this essentially Moderate bill but on the clearly Radical proposal to extend the suffrage to Negroes in the District of Columbia. A veto of the latter measure would have cost Johnson little and it might have been enough of a "deed" to convince doubting Democrats of his sincerity. But the District voting bill was held up in the parliamentary complexities of the Senate, and Johnson had to take his stand on the Freedmen's Bureau bill.

It was a stand which made a certain amount of sense politically—and it was the only stand possible for a President who hoped for re-election. Without a veto he knew that he and his party would almost certainly lose to the Democrats in 1868. With a veto, Johnson calculated that he might maintain a coalition of the center, composed of Moderate Republicans, War Democrats, and Southerners, and he might even profit by reading Sumner, Stevens, and a handful of other articulate Radicals from the party, just as Lincoln had gained by the Frémont defection in 1864. Such a plan, however, miscarried, for two weighty reasons. The first was the obvious fact that the Democrats in 1866 were in a stronger position, both numerically and psychologically, than they had been in 1864, when their Southern wing had been out of the Union and opposition to Lincoln could be equated with hostility to the nation itself. The second—less obvious to Johnson himself, and indeed to most historians as well—was a misreading of the basis and extent of the differences between the Moderate and Radical factions of the Republican party. To an examination of that issue the following chapter will be devoted.

II

THE
CONGRESSIONAL
EQUATION

WHEN MRS. JULIA WARD HOWE, ALREADY FAMOUS FOR HER "Battle Hymn of the Republic," visited Washington during the Civil War, she felt snubbed because her old friend Charles Sumner failed to call on her. Accidentally encountering her on the street, the Senator showed no remorse for his neglect but remarked languidly that he had "been engrossed so long by grand public questions" that he had "quite lost all interest in individuals." Promptly Mrs. Howe retorted that she was glad to hear of his progress, for she had not known that even the Almighty had "reached that point *yet*."

For generations historians have chuckled over Mrs. Howe's wit, but, without attempting to emulate Sumner's detachment in every way, I suggest that his attitude has some value for the student of Reconstruction. Perhaps we have all been too much interested in individuals. Recognizing that the road to reunion was surveyed by the Republicans in Congress, historians have devoted much attention to the individual leaders of that body. There has been much pen-swinging about even the most personal and eccentric aspects of their behavior— Thaddeus Stevens' alleged fondness for a mulatto mistress; Zachariah Chandler's demonstrable passion for liquor; Benjamin F. Butler's supposed gravitational attraction for silver spoons; and all the rest. Biography has its value, but the biographies of these Reconstruction leaders do not add up to any consistent interpretation of the age. From them, as we have seen, no historian has been able to construct a tenable thesis which will serve to distinguish Radical Republicans in terms of personality, ideology, geographical origins, or social and economic status from their Moderate counterparts.

Once we leave this circle of well-known and much-studied leaders, we confront the fact that the majority of the members of Congress, the men who actually passed the laws which determined the Reconstruction process, are almost total blanks: George W. Anderson, of Missouri; Abraham A. Barker, of Pennsylvania; John Bidwell, of California; and the rest of the dreary roll call. Lest this be read as a plea for graduate students to do more and more research on less and less consequential politicians, let it be said at once that not even the most enthusiastic state or local historian can resurrect most of these disembodied spirits. We cannot even rely upon the proverbial loquacity of Congressmen for further light on these forgotten men. During the four months in 1864 while the House of Representatives was considering the Davis Reconstruction bill (later the Wade-Davis bill), which surely posed most acutely the dilemmas of Reconstruction and the difficulties that lay ahead between executive and legislative branches of the government, only forty-one Congressmen of both parties even opened their mouths about the measure.

Since the leaders fall into no discernible pattern and since the followers are almost unknown, perhaps the time has come for the Reconstruction historian to emulate Sumner's olympian remoteness and to cease being concerned with individuals. In studying Republican factionalism it might be helpful to forget about personality, rhetoric, motives, and popular repute of individual Congressmen. Instead, we may hope to find significance in their objective behavior patterns —i.e., in the way they voted—and to explain this behavior in terms of political forces.

I

It is not, as we have seen, easy to find objective criteria for separating Radical from Moderate Republicans during the Civil War years. During the Reconstruction period the party situation became more complex, because a few Republicans, like Edgar Cowan, James R. Doolittle, and Henry J. Raymond, became identified with President Johnson's policies and formed a separate, clearly recognizable group of Conservatives, falling somewhere between the Democrats and the Republicans. But their defection did little to make the line between Moderate and Radical Republicans in Congress clearer. The final votes even on such controversial measures as the Second Confiscation Act, the bill for the readmission of Arkansas, the 1866 Civil Rights bill, and the 1867 Reconstruction Act reveal only monolithic Republican solidarity in both houses. But, by working carefully through the congressional proceedings, we can point to preliminary roll calls on some of these measures, where the caucus rules were not in force, where the party whip was held in abeyance, and where it was thought permissible for Republicans to express their differences and to divide along factional lines.

The following roll-call analysis is confined to votes taken in the House of Representatives. In thus apparently neglecting the Senate, I have no desire to minimize the importance of that body, whose debates I have studied with care if not with pleasure, or to deny the existence of Republican factionalism there. But Senators are such prickly and egotistical persons that alliances among them tend to be short-lived. Moreover, the most important business of the upper house was often transacted in the secret meetings of the Republican caucus, of which no minutes were kept, and the public record of Senate proceedings published in the *Congressional Globe* is decidedly unrevealing. Finally, since the members of the Senate were indirectly elected for long terms, the upper house is not the best place to test the effect of constituents' influence upon legislative action.

I have found no one vote during the Civil War years which will serve as a clear-cut test of Radicalism, but during the sessions of the Thirty-Eighth Congress in 1864 and 1865 there were six House roll calls, often on small and even procedural matters, which, taken together, show patterns of bloc voting. Doubtless another historian might select a somewhat different series of preliminary test votes, but these six, all relating directly to Reconstruction issues, seem to me most sharply to define the factions:

(1) The vote, on May 4, 1864, on a proposal, sponsored by acknowledged Radicals, to add a preamble to the Davis Reconstruction bill (later the Wade-Davis bill) to the effect that Confederates had "no right to claim the mitigation of the extreme rights of war" and announcing that none of the states of the Confederacy could "be considered and treated as entitled to be represented in Congress, or to take any part in the political government of the Union." Moderate Republicans allied with Democrats to defeat the preamble (76–57).

(2) The vote, on December 13, 1864, on a motion to remove a bill for the reconstruction of Louisiana from the fairly Moderate House judiciary committee and give it to the special committee on the rebellious states, headed by the arch-

Radical, Henry Winter Davis. The vote was a tie (66–66), with many abstentions, and the Speaker broke it by recording his vote against the proposal.

(3) The vote, on January 17, 1865, to postpone for two weeks further consideration of a Radical-sponsored bill for the reconstruction of Louisiana and other Southern states. Moderate Republicans joined Democrats to secure the delay (103–34).

(4) The vote, on February 21, 1865, to table this Reconstruction bill favored by the Radicals. Moderate Republicans and Democrats united in an attempt to kill the bill (91–64).

(5) The immediately subsequent roll call to table a motion to reconsider this vote on the general Reconstruction bill. Again the Radicals were defeated (92–57).

(6) The vote, on February 22, 1865, to table a bill providing that constitutional conventions in the Confederate states should be elected by loyal whites and Negroes who had served in the Union armies, to the exclusion of all Southern whites who had held civil or military office "under the rebel usurpation" and of all who had "voluntarily borne arms against the United States." Once again the Radicals were defeated by a Moderate-Democratic alliance (80–65).

No one of these votes, it should be repeated, is a sure index of a Congressman's identification with one faction or another. Even a composite tabulation has to be used with care, for indubitable Radicals, like Thaddeus Stevens and George W. Julian, sure that all the Reconstruction proposals before the Thirty-Eighth Congress were milk-and-water measures and confident that the Thirty-Ninth Congress would impose more rigorous conditions upon the South, had voting records on these six measures rather like those of conservative Northern Democrats. Nevertheless, the six votes taken together do select out a considerable number of House Republicans who favored congressional, rather than presidential, control over the Reconstruction process and who looked toward punitive action against the Southern rebels. Ten House Republicans voted the Radical line on all of these six measures. Twenty-nine others agreed with the Radical position on all but one of these votes, and eleven more disagreed with the Radicals on only two of the votes. These fifty Congressmen, then, may be taken as the core of Republican Radicalism in the House of Representatives during the last year of the Civil War.[2]

To determine party and factional groupings in the House of Representatives during the Reconstruction period, I have made roll-call tabulations of every vote, however apparently trivial or technical, recorded during the second session of the Thirty-Ninth Congress (1866–67) on all resolutions or bills relating to the reorganization of the South.[3] Of these six proved significant:

(1) The vote, on December 4, 1866, which approved the resolution offered by John M. Broomall, of Pennsylvania, requiring the committee on territories to look into the expediency of reporting a bill that would establish territorial governments, with universal manhood suffrage, in all the former Confederate states except Tennessee. Since the resolution asked only for an inquiry and not for specific action, it was supported by 106 Radical and Moderate Republicans and by one Democrat; 8 Conservatives joined 29 Democrats in opposing it.

(2) The vote, on January 28, 1867, to refer a drastic Reconstruction bill urged by Thaddeus Stevens, who would have disfranchised most Southern whites and given the vote to the Negroes, back to the Joint Committee of Fifteen on Reconstruction, where it would in all probability languish until the

[2] For the voting records of all Republican Representatives on these measures and the names of the Radicals, see Appendixes I and II.

[3] See Appendix III.

end of the Thirty-Ninth Congress. John A. Bingham, of Ohio, the leading Moderate Republican in the House, sponsored the motion to refer, and fifty other Moderate Republicans and Conservatives joined him in voting with the Democrats to defeat the Stevens proposal (88–65).

(3) The vote, on February 11, 1867, on ordering the main question—i.e., on cutting off further debate and moving toward a final vote—on the bill introduced by Thomas D. Eliot, of Massachusetts, to provide for the reconstruction of Louisiana. Eliot's proposal was drastic, and it had strong Radical backing, but since the provisional government of Louisiana had shown itself so unable or unwilling to protect its Negro citizens, many Moderate Republicans supported the measure. Twenty-one Moderate Republicans and Conservatives joined with the Democrats in an effort to protract the debate, but the motion was carried over their opposition (84–59).

(4) The vote, on February 13, 1867, on ordering the main question—again cutting off further debate and delay—on James G. Blaine's Moderate proposal to refer the military Reconstruction bill, which Stevens was now advocating, to the committee on the judiciary, where Moderate amendments would be added. Moderate Republicans, Conservatives, and twenty Democrats favored cutting off debate; fifty-seven other Republicans followed Stevens in joining the remaining Democrats in an effort to prolong the debate. The Moderates won (85–78).

(5) The subsequent vote, on the same day, on Blaine's motion itself. Fifty-two Moderate Republicans and Conservatives joined with seventeen Democrats to send the military bill to the judiciary committee for amendment, but they were defeated by a coalition of seventy-one Radical Republicans and twenty-three Democrats (69–94).

(6) The final vote, also taken the same day, on the adop-

tion of the Stevens version of the military Reconstruction bill. Thirteen Conservatives joined the Democrats in opposing final passage, but they were overwhelmed by the united Moderate and Radical Republican vote (109–55).

Taken together, these six votes select out seventy-two Republican Representatives in the Thirty-Ninth Congress who could be generally relied upon to support Radical legislation directed at the South.[4]

II

To study these fifty Republican Radicals of 1864-65 and these seventy-two Republican Radicals of 1866-67 in the way historians usually analyze groups is thoroughly disheartening. No obvious personal or social characteristics united them or distinguished them from other Republican Congressmen. They were not notably different in ethnic background, geographical origin, previous political affiliation, or age from the non-Radical Republican Representatives in the same Congress. Far too little is known, and can be known, about most of these Radicals to warrant any generalization as to their social-economic status or personality type, but the few who have been studied by historians fall into no single pattern.

Voting together on measures relating to the South, the Negro, and Reconstruction was the one bond which held these Radicals together. They tended consistently to vote together on such issues over a considerable period of time. Of the fifty Radicals of 1864-65, forty-one were still serving in the House of Representatives two years later, and three out of

[4] Republican Representatives are classified by factions in Appendix IV. Since my purpose here is to develop a general explanation of factionalism, I have in the following pages discussed these Radicals as a single group. As the next chapter shows, one can distinguish three subcategories of Radicals—Independent Radicals, Stevens Radicals, and Ultra Radicals—but the differences among these were over relatively minor, tactical matters.

TABLE I

Votes of Radical Congressmen of 1864–65
on 1867 Reconstruction Legislation

Of 10 Republicans who voted Radical on all 6 test roll calls in 1864–65:

    7 voted with the Radicals in 1867

    1 voted with the Moderates in 1867

    1 joined no recognized faction in 1867

    1 was not re-elected (replaced by another Republican who voted Radical in 1867)

Of 29 Republicans who voted Radical on 5 of 6 test roll calls in 1864–65:

    18 voted with the Radicals in 1867

    3 voted with the Moderates in 1867

    1 voted with the Conservatives in 1867

    1 was an absentee in 1867

    6 were not re-elected (replaced by 2 Radicals, 1 Moderate, 2 Democrats, and 1 absentee in 1867)

Of 11 Republicans who voted Radical on 4 of 6 test roll calls in 1864–65:

    6 voted with the Radicals in 1867

    1 voted with the Moderates in 1867

    1 joined no recognized faction in 1867

    1 was an absentee in 1867

    2 were not re-elected (replaced by 1 Moderate and 1 Democrat in 1867)

four of them continued to vote Radical (see Table I). Since in the 1860's the Representative's term of service tended to be short and precarious, this record of continuity inevitably provokes the speculation that there might be some connection between the relative degree of security which these Congressmen felt in their office and their Radical voting record.

A study of the election returns proves that, in fact, the fifty Radicals in the Thirty-Eighth Congress (1864–65) were elected by overwhelming majorities, having received on the average 58.3 per cent of the vote in their districts even in 1862, the disastrous year when military defeats and Lincoln's emancipation policies nearly cost the Republican party control of the House. Their districts continued to be heavily Republican long after 1862, since all but three of them elected these same Representatives or other Republicans in both 1864 and 1866. It is tempting to derive from such figures a new formula to explain Republican factionalism: Radicalism was a function of party strength. Or, to put it less technically, one might predict that the more heavily a district voted Republican, the more surely its Representative would support Radical measures in Congress.

It would be gratifying to report that my analysis of voting statistics, which I have calculated for every congressional district for every election during the Civil War and Reconstruction era, confirms this simple formula, but, unfortunately, such is not the case. The seventy-two Republicans who can be identified as Radicals in the 1866–67 Congress had been elected in 1864 by an average vote of 59.3 per cent [5]— but the thirty-two recognizable Moderate Republicans in the same session had received an average vote in that election of 59.2 per cent. On first trial, therefore, a definition of Radicalism in terms of constituency strength seems no more successful than the economic, geographical, psychological, or other interpretations of Republican factionalism.

But, upon reflection, perhaps I should have expected to encounter what V. O. Key used to call "melancholy experience with the eccentricities of data," which resolutely refuse to fall into a simple pattern. It would be unreasonable to hope that all election data in a country so broad and diverse as the United States would conform to a single formula. Moreover, that formula implies a degree of correla-

[5] In a few states Congressmen were chosen in odd, rather than even, years, and in these cases I have used 1865 election returns.

tion between constituents' attitudes and a Congressman's voting that is contrary to our everyday experience. We know that many Representatives—in the 1860's as well as in the 1960's—owed their seats not to their votes or speeches on great national issues but to their skill in securing federal contracts for factories in their districts, in winning appropriations to improve local rivers and harbors, and the like. Other Congressmen were elected because of their ethnic or religious affiliations. In still other cases districts chose Representatives for none of these reasons but because they were war heroes.

No doubt many of even these Congressmen did try to make their votes on Reconstruction issues conform to the wishes of the voters in their districts, but it was hard always to know what those wishes were. Since the Civil War so closely and directly affected most Northern families, there was an unusual amount of public interest in the general issues of Reconstruction, but only a minority of voters could have held decided opinions on specific legislative proposals—say, on the merits of James M. Ashley's proposed Reconstruction plan as compared with those of Thaddeus Stevens' bill. Though a Congressman tried to learn both the desires of this articulate minority and the general preferences of his constituents by reading his mail, by studying the newspapers published in his district, and by talking with the voters on his occasional visits home, he could never be really sure he was reflecting the will of the majority.

For some Congressmen the opinions of their constituents were not a major consideration. Many of the Representatives who voted on the 1867 Reconstruction Act were lame-ducks, Congressmen who either had not stood for re-election the previous fall or who had been defeated. These, it would be only reasonable to expect, would care less about what the voters back home wanted than did the Congressmen who had just been re-elected and who might hope for additional terms of office in the future. It is significant that of the Republicans who supported Bingham's Moderate resolution in 1867, which sent Stevens' Radical Reconstruction bill to its death in committee, one in four was ending his service in the House, while only one in eight of the Radicals was retiring. Even more instructive is the fact that three-fifths of the twenty-five Republican Representatives who abstained from voting in this clear test of factions had not been re-elected; they had the independence of judgment which can be exhibited by the politicians who aspire to nothing.

A Representative who hoped for higher political office might also show himself indifferent to the voice of his constituency. If James A. Garfield, re-elected in 1866 by 71.3 per cent of the votes in his Ohio district, or Nathaniel P. Banks, chosen by 74.9 per cent of his Massachusetts constituency, hoped to become President or Vice President, he had to reckon with the same pressure that had pushed both Lincoln and Johnson into a Moderate, or even a Conservative, position. No man could hope to gain the Republican nomination for national office, much less to win the election itself, unless his record was Moderate enough for independents and some Democrats, who together formed the majority of the nation's voting population, to support him.

Because of these considerations, which can only be evaluated on a local level, it is best to study the relationship between Republican factional affiliation and voting strength in individual states, or regional groups of states. From the critical state of New York, where the Democrats elected the governor in 1862 and won seventeen of the state's thirty-one seats in the House of Representatives, there were only two Radicals in the 1864-65 Congress. Both of these had been elected, even in the black year of 1862, by over 57 per cent of their districts' voters. By 1864, with the worst of the war over, voters began returning to their normal allegiances, and Republicanism was resurgent in New York. Even though the two parties were closely balanced in voting for national and state-wide offices, the Republicans regained a majority of the congressional delegation, in many instances by very large majorities. Radicalism increased along with Republican voting strength, and by 1866–67 three New York Representatives belonged to the Radical faction, while five were Moderates and three were Conservatives.

A graph of the voting record of these individual New York districts (see Figure I) strikingly shows that Radicals usually represented the most heavily Republican districts in the state, that Moderates came from marginal districts where some Democratic support was necessary for victory, and that Conservatives were the temporary Congressmen from districts whose normal affiliation was Democratic. A chart showing the average vote received by Republican candidates in these three kinds of districts (see Figure II) even more impressively reinforces this thesis.

Pennsylvania election returns (see Figure III) generally fall into the same pattern as those of New York. The Ninth Pennsylvania District, which consistently cast the highest percentage of Republican votes throughout the era, sent none other than Thaddeus Stevens himself to Congress, while the two Moderate districts were always marginally Republican. There was, however, an important difference between the pattern of Pennsylvania and New York voting. The former was a notably Radical state, and Congressmen from many of its weaker Republican districts tended to support Radical measures. Representative Leonard Myers, for example, received on the average only 51.1 per cent of the votes in his Third Pennsylvania District, but he stalwartly voted alongside Thaddeus Stevens. In New York, one can hardly doubt, such a Congressman would have been a Moderate, or even Conservative. The key to the difference lies in the fact that

Figure I

Percentage of Votes Received by Republican Candidates in New York Congressional Districts, 1862–68 *

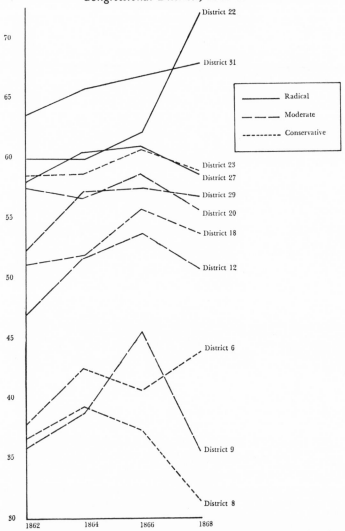

* Districts are classified according to votes of their Representatives in the 1866–67 session of Congress. Districts whose Representatives were not identified with any Republican faction, who were absentees, or who were Democrats in 1867 are not shown.

Figure II

Average Percentage of Votes Received by Republican Candidates in Radical, Moderate, and Conservative New York Districts, 1862–68 *

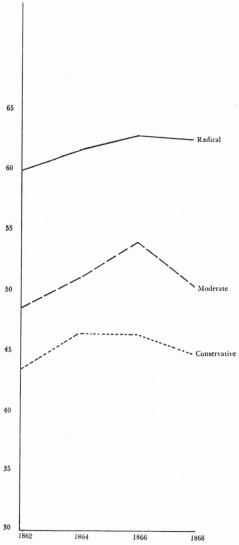

* Districts are classified according to votes of their Representatives in the 1866–67 session of Congress.

Figure III

Percentage of Votes Received by Republican Candidates in Pennsylvania Congressional Districts, 1862–68 *

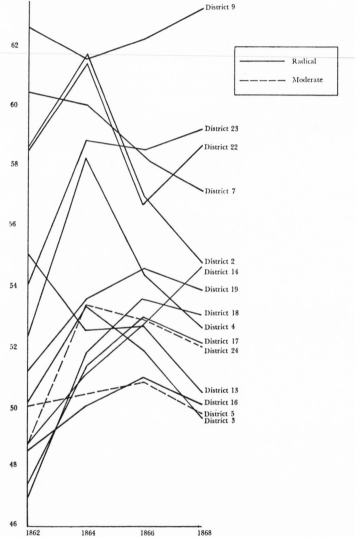

* Districts are classified according to votes of their Representatives in the 1866–67 session of Congress. Districts whose Representatives were Democratic or who were Republican abstainers are not shown.

the Democratic organization in Pennsylvania was feebler than that in New York, while Pennsylvania Republicans were well organized, disciplined, and financed. As a result, the Republican Congressman from the Keystone State felt a greater security in office than did his New York counterpart. Nine of the Pennsylvania districts elected Republican Representatives in every election from 1862 to 1868, and seven others chose Republicans in all but one of these elections. Representative Myers' margins might be small, year after year, but he could have a high degree of confidence that he would be repeatedly returned to office.

The election returns from the states of the Middle West (Ohio, Indiana, Illinois, Michigan, Wisconsin, Minnesota, Iowa, and Kansas) generally correspond to those of New York and Pennsylvania. Since most of these were strongly Republican states, one would expect to find a strong preponderance of Radicals among their Congressmen. In fact, fifteen of the fifty Radicals of the 1864–65 Congress came from this region, as did thirty-one of the seventy-two in the 1866–67 session, which contained only twelve Moderates from the Middle West and only four Conservatives. These three groups of Middle Western Republican Congressmen received strikingly different degrees of support in the 1864 elections. The successful Radical candidate in that year won, on the average, 57.8 per cent of the total vote in his district; the Moderate received 55.7 per cent;[6] and the Conservative had only 51.7 per cent.

Within any single Middle Western state the symmetry of this pattern is likely to be marred because of circumstances

---

[6] The votes of James A. Garfield and J. F. Farnsworth have been omitted from this calculation. In the 1864–65 Congress Garfield voted with the Radicals, but two years later he was thinking of state or national offices and felt compelled to be a Moderate. Farnsworth's voting record was erratic. Though he supported Bingham's motion on January 28, 1867, in most other respects he agreed with the Radicals.

peculiar to individual districts and to individual candidates, yet a glance at the Indiana Republican election percentage for 1864 (see Table II) shows that, in a rough way, Radical Congressmen from that state tended to come from areas of great Republican constituency strength, while Representatives from doubtful districts were usually Moderates or Conservatives.

TABLE II

Percentage of Votes Received
By Indiana Republican Representatives in 1864

Radicals in 1867	*Percentage*
G. W. Julian	68.7
Ebenezer Dumont	63.4
G. S. Orth	52.2
J. H. Farquhar	50.1*
Moderate in 1867	
Ralph Hill	51.8
Conservatives in 1867	
T. N. Stillwell	53.8
J. H. Defrees	51.0
Representatives not voting on 4 or more of 6 test roll calls	
Schuyler Colfax (*Speaker*)	52.6
H. D. Washburn	50.0

It is, at first thought, rather a surprise to find that votes in the New England states reflect this same tendency. They were, after all, securely Republican and had few marginal districts. Massachusetts, for example, elected only Republicans to Congress from 1862 through 1870, and the weakest Republican in 1864 received 62.3 per cent of the votes in his district. Yet, aside from Banks, who had presidential aspirations, the Massachusetts Representatives with the strongest constituency support were Radicals, while those with the

* Farquhar can best be characterized as an Independent Radical (see Chapter III, below). Though he sometimes supported Radical positions, he voted for J. A. Bingham's motion on January 28, 1867.

least voted Moderate (see Table III). It would be misleading to consider the three Moderate Massachusetts seats doubtful in the same sense that districts were marginal in New York or Indiana, yet two of them, which included the city of Boston, gave Lincoln only a minority vote in 1860 and supported a Democratic gubernatorial candidate two years later. In these districts there seems to have been much crossing of party lines in the congressional elections by Democrats who realized that their party had little chance to win and who, therefore, supported Republicans known to be Moderates.

TABLE III

Percentage of Votes Received
By Massachusetts Representatives in 1864

Radicals in 1867	Percentage
T. D. Eliot	82.7
W. B. Washburn	81.4
J. B. Alley	75.8
John Baldwin	74.8
G. S. Boutwell	68.9
Moderates in 1867	
H. L. Dawes	64.7
Samuel Hooper	64.0
A. H. Rice	62.3
Conservative in 1867	
N. P. Banks	80.0

Thus, though there were a great many individual and local eccentricities, voting behavior in New England, the Middle States, and the Middle West conformed to a general pattern. When a district, over a long series of elections, showed itself to be doubtful or only marginally Republican, its Representative frequently tended to vote with the Moderate or Conservative blocs in Congress. But when there was a consistent degree of high Republican strength in a district, its Congressman usually belonged to the Radical faction of the party.

III

It is not hard to account for this ratio between security in office and Radicalism. A Congressman from a stalwartly Republican district or state was aware that he owed little to his national party and less to the President. In many cases he had joined the Republican party before Abraham Lincoln, and he generally ran ahead of the presidential candidate in both 1860 and 1864. In his view Andrew Johnson, a lifelong Southern Democrat, was even less entitled than Lincoln to set policy for the party which he accidentally headed.

To be sure, even a Congressman from a safely Republican district or state looked to the President for patronage, but in the early months of his administration Lincoln tied his own hands by requiring that Representatives be consulted about appointments in their own districts and he later extended this rule to cover the small army of internal revenue appointees created under the tax law of 1862. In any case, after 1862, most of the choice jobs had already been distributed, and the Congressman's insatiable appetite for new patronage triumphed over his transient memory of past favors. The advent of Andrew Johnson did little to make him more dependent upon the White House. Severely limited by his need to keep the National Union coalition intact, Johnson, as we have seen, made few removals for political reasons in 1865–66, and those few served more to insure the bitter hostility of the displaced than the loyalty of the new officeholders.

The secure Republican Congressman, in short, felt more certain of his base of power than did the President. Unless he aspired to national office, he had no need to be Moderate, for he required no support from the independents or the Democrats. Nor did he have any need to follow the President's course, for his own power stemmed from his seniority on important congressional committees. To be sure, not all Congressmen from overwhelmingly Republican districts desired to flout the President's will or to espouse harsh Reconstruction measures. A Representative like Thomas A. Jenckes, whose Rhode Island district voted 99.0 per cent Republican in 1865 and 97.7 per cent Republican in 1867, was so well entrenched that he could follow his own ideas, without much regard to possible disaffection of constituents. But most of the leading Radicals in both houses occupied unassailably secure Republican seats—Charles Sumner, Thaddeus Stevens, Zachariah Chandler, George W. Julian, and the rest.

Very different was the lot of the Republican Congressman from the doubtful district. Where the vote was almost evenly divided, he had to eschew Radicalism, whatever his own personal wishes and beliefs. The most thoughtful exponent of the Moderate position in the House was John A. Bingham, who was fully aware that his Ohio district could easily go Democratic, since his own average vote in the elections from 1862 through 1870 was only 50.6 per cent of the total. Bitterly he protested against Radical proposals "for universal suffrage among . . . women and colored citizens, and for confiscation, banishment, and the disfranchisement of all others without trial—and for the removal of the President by Joint Resolution." Begging his fellow Republicans not to commit "an act of political Suicide," he warned: "Any such folly on our part will inevitably throw the whole country into the hands of the opposition alias the late rebels."

Even had there been no pressure from his own district, such a Representative would have felt obliged to support the President, who, as we have seen, was compelled to be a Moderate. The Congressman from the doubtful district often had only a brief tenure, and he could not normally expect to have much power in the House committees. His continuance in office often depended upon presidential backing,

sometimes by way of the suppression of hostile newspapers
or even the use of Federal troops to keep his Democratic opponents from the polls. Powerful too for such Congressmen
was the pull of the presidential coat-tail. In New York, for
instance, Lincoln's race for re-election in 1864 helped both
Radical and Moderate Republican candidates in the same
degree, but, as Table IV shows, the increase in strength was
only a welcome addition to large majorities for the Radicals
while to many Moderate candidates it made the difference
between success and failure.

TABLE IV

Average Percentage of Votes
Received by New York Republican Candidates
for Congress, 1862 and 1864*

Year	Conservatives	Moderates	Radicals
1862	43.3	48.6	60.3
1864	46.6	51.0	61.8

The need for the marginal Republican Congressman to
look to the President, therefore, overruled considerations of
personality or ideology. The case of Representative Owen
Lovejoy of Illinois, the brother of an early antislavery
martyr, is instructive. During the 1850's there had been few
Republicans in the House more vituperative toward the
South and more positive that the social system of that region
had to be radically reorganized. But after the 1860 census,
Illinois, like many other states, was redistricted, and Lovejoy's once safe seat became doubtful. Frightened, the Illinois
Congressman put aside his fear that President Lincoln was
too slow, too lenient, too soft on the South and, through a
friend, made a "delicate request" for Presidential endorsement. "He has a fierce battle in his district," the intermediary

* Districts classified according to Representatives' position on 1867 legislation.

wrote Lincoln on October 21, 1862, "but thinks that a line which he might not use in the newspapers but to exhibit to a few of your friends would do him great service." With the President's backing Lovejoy won re-election in 1862 by a majority of only fifty-six votes, and he became one of the President's most stalwart supporters in the House, although he continued from time to time to urge faster action. In Professor Williams' carefully documented compilation of Radical assaults upon the President, the last anti-Lincoln item from Congressman Lovejoy is dated June, 1862; thereafter, the facts of political life controlled and he became Lincoln's man. When Lovejoy died in 1864, the President praised him as his "most generous friend," who deserved to be enduringly remembered "in the hearts of those who love liberty, unselfishly, for all men."

Other Republicans from marginal districts felt the same pressures toward moderation on issues of slavery and Reconstruction. Isaac N. Arnold, who, next to Lovejoy, received the smallest majority of any Illinois Republican candidate for Congress in 1862, became one of the few Congressmen who early and enthusiastically urged Lincoln's re-election, and after the assassination he wrote a warmly admiring biography of the President. Bradley F. Granger, elected to Congress in 1860 by the smallest majority of any Republican candidate in Michigan, sought vainly to avert defeat in his re-election campaign by becoming one of the few Republican Representatives to vote against confiscation measures. More successful was Joseph H. Defrees, who, after the Tenth Indiana District went Democratic in 1862, recognized that a Republican could win only if he attracted support outside of his party regulars. Though Indiana Radicals from their safe seats scorned him as an old fogy, his Conservative views won him election in 1864.

In the Reconstruction years as well leading Moderates and

Conservatives came from marginal and doubtful districts. The case of John A. Bingham has already been noted. Even more striking is that of Henry J. Raymond, the editor of the New York *Times,* who became Andrew Johnson's chief spokesman and defender in the House. The fact that Raymond was elected in 1864 only because New York Democrats in his Sixth District were divided and that no Republican candidate for Congress received more than 47 per cent of the vote in that district in any election from 1860 through 1870 explains much about the sources of Conservative Republicanism.

IV

In arguing that a Congressman's Radicalism during Reconstruction varied in proportion to his political security in his district, I am, of course, making an implicit judgment that most Republican voters were themselves Radicals, in the sense that they desired the abolition of slavery, the reorganization of Southern society, and the perpetuation of Republican control of the national government. No student who has studied the Republican newspapers of the period and the unpublished correspondence of Republican leaders can doubt that this was the case, at least up to the time when Johnson was impeached. It would be easy to compile an anthology of letters in the same vein as that of a Ravenna, Ohio, Republican to Representative Garfield in February, 1867: "The delay of Congress in coming to any agreement is trying the patience of the people very much. The masses sympathize with Stevens more than men in Washington think. . . . Don't be afraid of the people. They are ahead of Congress now, as they were during the war, when the administration of Mr. Lincoln was timidly halting, and afraid to touch the *hallowed* institution of slavery!" Regardless of their personal convictions, therefore, those Congressmen repeatedly elected by Republican votes alone were pushed by their constituents into becoming increasingly Radical.

On the other hand, if the Moderate Republican Congressman's course during Reconstruction can be related to his need to secure broader support in his doubtful district, it is legitimate to ask whether he really disagreed on issues and principles with the Radicals in his party or whether he was subordinating his true beliefs to expediency. To this question no definitive answer can be given, for we know, and can know, much too little about what most Congressmen truly believed. Doubtless in many cases a circular process was at work: doubtful districts ran Republican candidates known to have Moderate views, in order to secure Democratic support; Congressmen from such districts supported Moderate positions because they had to woo marginal voters.

It is perhaps permissible to speculate that, had all Republicans been equally free from the necessity of playing to a bipartisan constituency, the ideological differences between Moderates and Radicals might not have amounted to a great deal. Certainly historians have tended to polarize these differences to an unwarranted extent. It is instructive to remember that Moderate Senator William Pitt Fessenden, of Maine, objected to the final version of the 1867 Reconstruction Act because, he said, "it did not go far enough." The "gentlemen who glory in the name of radical," he took waspish pleasure in pointing out, "are not quite so radical on that subject as I am. . . ." Similarly, it is chastening to note that Bingham's adherence to the Fourteenth Amendment as a truly Moderate plan of Reconstruction had some decidedly Radical overtones. Asked how, in view of Southern refusal to accept that amendment, it could become part of the Constitution, Bingham replied that there was no need for it to be ratified except "by three fourths of the organized and represented States"—i.e., by the North and the West, without consulting the South; this was precisely the position maintained by Radical Charles Sumner in the Senate. But when colleagues suggested to Bingham that the Supreme Court might not sustain such a partial ratification of an amendment, the Ohio Moderate took a breath-taking step even beyond the most Radical in his party by suggesting that Congress should first curtail the Court's jurisdiction and then procure "a further constitutional amendment . . . , which will defy judicial usurpation by . . . the abolition of the tribunal itself."

Certainly as Republican voting strength increased between 1862 and 1864, the number of Radical Republicans in Congress, as we have noted, grew proportionately. There were further additions to the Radical ranks after the elections of 1866, when Southern failure to guarantee minimal rights to the Negroes and Johnson's ill-conceived "swing around the circle" in support of his policy resulted in larger Republican majorities throughout the North. In the case of individual Congressmen the transformation from Moderate to Radical was neither immediate nor complete, but it is suggestive that Bingham, who thought the Civil Rights bill of 1866 unconstitutional and took his stand on the Fourteenth Amendment, came out for Negro suffrage in 1867 and the year after became one of the seven House impeachment managers at Andrew Johnson's trial. There was, therefore, a certain warped wisdom in Montgomery Blair's view that Republican factional fights, such as those which led up to the adoption of the 1867 Reconstruction Act, were all play-acting, part of a plan to throw dust in President Johnson's eyes "by having Bingham . . . *pretending* to make war on Stephens [*sic*]."

But the factional war within the Republican party was, in fact, no pretense, even if the basis of the factions was political necessity rather than ideology. Moderates had to check extreme Radical proposals or be defeated in the districts they represented. To the Radicals, on the other hand, the Moderates seemed a dead weight, the more onerous because these fellow party members ought to know better. The history of Reconstruction legislation is the story of the tug of war between these two groups, and, as we shall see in the next chapter, it, like the basis of factionalism, can best be analyzed in quantitative, almost mechanistic, terms.

III

THE
PENDULUM OF
LEGISLATION

"I WAS A CONSERVATIVE IN THE LAST SESSION OF THIS Congress," Thaddeus Stevens told a laughing group of admirers when the House of Representatives reassembled in December, 1866, "but I mean to be a Radical henceforth." Recognizing the old man's grim humor, historians have frequently accepted Stevens' statement as an indication of the new mood of the Republicans in the memorable second session of the Thirty-Ninth Congress, which ran from December 3, 1866, to March 4, 1867. With overwhelming majorities in both Houses, the Republicans in this session passed the Tenure of Office Act, depriving the President of control over civilian employees of the national government, an Army Appropriations Act, stripping him so far as possible of control over the army, and the Reconstruction Act of March 2, 1867, placing all the former Confederate states except Tennessee under military rule. The history of this session of the Congress, according to J. G. Randall, was the story of how the Radicals bullied "the large moderate majority of the Republican party" into "adopting new and severe measures toward the South." Its record of legislation, James Ford Rhodes thought, was largely due to the "able and despotic parliamentary leadership" of Thaddeus Stevens.

I

It is easy to see how a historian could arrive at this—or at almost any other—interpretation of the origins of the 1867 Reconstruction Act, for the protracted and turgid debates which occupied most of the time of one, or sometimes both, of the houses of Congress for over eight weeks were so involved as to confuse even some of the Congressmen who participated in them. No fewer than eighty-four Representatives and thirty-eight Senators felt impelled to speak on the Reconstruction bill, and some of them spoke frequently and at great length. The whole debate was marked by intricate parliamentary maneuvers of great technical complexity, and, as evening sessions dragged on until long after midnight, a good number of Congressmen appear to have found relief from the tension in the bars conveniently located in the Capitol lobbies. So rowdy did the Representatives become at one time that Ebenezer Dumont, of Indiana, had the clerk read to the House a notice posted by a Washington hotel-keeper on his dining room door: "Members of Congress will go to the table first, and then the gentlemen. Rowdies and blackguards must not mix with the Congressmen, as it is hard to tell one from the other."

Many of the speeches, as one Representative confessed, were mostly not intended "to enlighten the members here nor to produce any conviction upon the minds of gentlemen . . . in this House" but to impress constituents. Some of the

Congressmen wrote out, and even rehearsed, their speeches, which were bedizened with quotations from Shakespeare, Milton, and scores of lesser poets and were full of invocations of the Gracchi, Cincinnatus, Seneca, and Cicero. Others, as the record all too clearly shows, preferred to rely upon "the spontaneous flow of ideas . . . and on the inspiration of the moment." Much of the debate had little to do with the merits of the specific legislation under consideration, and it tended on the one side to drift off the subject into denunciations of the despotism of the Republican party or, on the other, into accusations that Andrew Johnson and the Northern Democrats were traitors. Senator Lyman Trumbull, of Illinois, used a good part of one evening session to defend the war record of one General Paine, incidentally mentioned in another Senator's speech as having looted Kentucky. Senator James Doolittle spent most of a morning presumably dedicated to debate of the Reconstruction bill in refuting the right of the Wisconsin legislature either to instruct him how to vote or to ask for his resignation. After pouring over the 2,005 pages of close, triple-column type which immortalize the debates of this one session of Congress, it is easy to share the sentiments of a Senator who protested, when a motion of his was declared out of order: "I think from the range of this debate almost anything is in order."

Even when Congressmen stuck to the subject, their arguments were not always easy to follow. Frequently they dealt with constitutional problems of almost metaphysical subtlety: What was a state? Was it the territory, the people, or the government of an area—or all three? Were the Southern states in or out of the Union? If, as the Republicans had claimed throughout the Civil War, states had no right to secede and had, therefore, always been in the Union, by what constitutional authority could Congress regulate their elections or exclude their chosen representatives from its halls? Had the Southern states committed suicide? Were they in a state of suspended animation? Or were they conquered territories? Was the United States still at war with these Southern states, or was it at peace—or was there, according to international law, still a third possibility, that of *bello cessante?* After exploring these arguments, the historian can but sympathize with Senator John Conness, of California, who, after weeks of debate, lamented: "I do not know just exactly what is in controversy here, although I have been listening for some time. The arguments seem to be drawn so fine that it has almost passed from my perception."

Despite their limitations—or perhaps despite their lack of limitation—the congressional debates that led up to the 1867 Reconstruction Act will repay a fresh, close study, which, if combined with an analysis of the roll-call votes, suggests the inadequacy of older interpretations of this momentous piece of legislation. A day-by-day reading of the *Congressional Globe* shows that when the second session of the Thirty-Ninth Congress opened in December, 1866, the Republican party was badly divided over the necessity for further Reconstruction legislation. To be sure, the Radical wing of the party had been strengthened by its overwhelming victory in the recent congressional election, for, as we have seen, the Radicalism of an individual Congressman tended to be proportionate to the Republican strength in his constituency. Nevertheless, there were still many Moderate Republicans, especially from closely divided states like New York and Ohio, who had just won re-election by pledging that the Southern states would be readmitted as soon as they ratified the proposed Fourteenth Amendment, which the previous session of this Congress had submitted to the states.

Though eager for new and harsher measures to impose upon the South, veteran Radical leaders were unsure of their strength during the early part of the new session, and their less experienced followers vainly "waited month after month for some of these old and experienced legislators to bring forward something upon the subject of reconstruction." Aware that he could not muster a majority in the Joint Committee of Fifteen on Reconstruction, Stevens, the chairman, refused to call a committee meeting; consequently it could mature no new proposals. On December 19 Stevens did briefly bring up the Reconstruction bill favored by the Joint Committee the previous session "for the purpose of offering some amendments and having them printed," but since he had been instrumental in having this same proposal "kicked under the table" in April, 1866, it seems clear that he acted to forestall, rather than to expedite, debate.

After the Christmas holidays, however, Republicans were roused by news from the South. One by one, with overwhelming unanimity, the provisional governments President Johnson had set up in the former Confederate states rejected the proposed Fourteenth Amendment, and by March, 1867, all except Tennessee had acted negatively; their refusal, combined with similar action in Kentucky and Delaware, meant that three-fourths of the states would not accept the amendment. At the same time, the full effect of the Supreme Court's decision in the Milligan case, handed down in December, 1866, began to be felt. If the Milligan ruling applied to the South, martial law could no longer be enforced there, and army officers stationed in the former Confederate states were beginning to be harassed by suits brought in the local civil courts. President Johnson seemed to encourage the Southerners in their attitude of defiance, urging them to reject the Fourteenth Amendment and suggesting that there was doubt of the legality of the Congress itself, since it excluded from its membership representatives of ten states of the Union.

In light of these developments virtually all Republican Congressmen began to feel the need for passing some new

Reconstruction legislation—and for passing it quickly, since this Congress by law expired on March 4, 1867, and any bill passed less than ten days before that date could be killed by a pocket veto. Believing that at last the party was aroused enough to move, Stevens on January 3, 1867, started the debate by introducing a bill (technically a substitute for the Joint Committee's earlier proposal, which he had called up before the holidays) to require each of the unreconstructed states to adopt a new constitution guaranteeing that henceforth "all laws shall be impartial, without regard to language, race or former condition." In electing members to the state conventions which should draw up these constitutions and in subsequently voting to ratify or reject them, "all male citizens above the age of twenty-one years" should have the right to participate, except those who had held office under or voluntarily sworn allegiance to the Confederacy. These were "declared to have forfeited their citizenship" and were not "entitled to exercise the elective franchise or hold office until five years after they shall have filed their intention or desire to be reinvested with the right of citizenship." After each Southern state had taken these steps, Congress would consider the propriety of readmitting it to the Union.

II

In order to explain the extraordinarily complex legislative history of this proposal historians have tried to fathom the motives of the Congressmen who defended and who opposed it, to express their differences in terms of rival ideologies, or to account for their behavior by their social and economic status or their geographical origins. Since none of these interpretations, when critically examined, has proved altogether satisfactory, perhaps the time has come to attempt an entirely different approach to these congressional proceedings by resorting to the simple arithmetic of politics. In December, 1866, there were 192 members of the House of Representatives, where the Reconstruction legislation originated, but this number included Speaker Schuyler Colfax, who voted only in case of a tie, and twenty-two members, mostly lame-ducks, who were regularly absent. It usually required, therefore, eighty-five votes to pass a bill in the House, and, if the President vetoed it, 113 votes were needed to pass it over his objection. Forty-four of the regularly present members of the House were Democrats, and all but one of these voted together on most measures relating to the South. Not powerful enough to carry measures of their own or to defeat bills supported by the united Republican factions, these Democrats played the negative role of pointing out inconsistencies in Republican arguments and of ridiculing Republican protestations of high principles. "Talk to a Radical about justice!" sneered Representative T. E. Noell, of Missouri; "you had as well sing love-songs to a mantua-maker's dummy."

Only a limited number of political strategies were available to this small Democratic minority. They could support President Johnson and introduce lenient Reconstruction proposals of their own, but there was no chance that any of these could be adopted. They could join Moderate Republicans and Conservatives in an attempt to temper the sharpness of Radical proposals, and some, like Democratic Senator Reverdy Johnson, of Maryland, urged this course as the speediest way to restore the South. There was, however, a danger here, for Democrats recognized that the more moderate the Reconstruction legislation passed by the majority party, the more likelihood there was that it would divide the Southern whites and lead to the creation of a viable Republican party in the states of the former Confederacy. Consequently some Democrats preferred the dangerous game of

voting on preliminary tests with the Radicals to draft Reconstruction legislation as unpalatable as possible to the
Southern whites, then making a public record by opposing on
the final vote the very bills they had helped shape. Most
Democrats tried to combine these tactics, throwing their
weight sometime to the Moderates, sometime to the Radicals,
in an effort simultaneously to exacerbate Republican factional differences and to frustrate all legislation.

Frequently voting with these Democrats were thirteen
Representatives who had been elected in 1864 as Republicans
but whose support of the Johnson program of Reconstruction clearly marked them as Conservatives. Theirs was the
politics of nostalgia, a reflection, in part, of the fact that
nine of them had not been re-elected in 1866 and would
therefore retire at least temporarily from public life at the
end of the Thirty-Ninth Congress. In their speeches they
frequently lamented the past errors on the part of both Congress and the President, and they looked back with longing
to the days when, as they remembered them, Lincoln and his
party had worked as a team. Ever alert to newspaper rumors
that Johnson was softening in his hostility toward Congress,
they believed that, in time, they could work out "a solution,
in which the two Houses of Congress will agree, in which the
people of this country will sustain us, and in which the President of the United States will give us his support."

The remaining 112 voting members of the House were
regular Republicans. Though they had their differences, they
were united in a strong desire to continue the hegemony of
the Republican party, and they frequently pointed with pride
to the "sublime record" of their party in the past and begged
their colleagues to do nothing "that will dim the luster of
its immortal fame." Both Moderate and Radical Republicans
shared the conviction "that on the continued ascendancy of
that [Republican] party depends the safety of this great

nation." In consequence they looked with alarm upon the readmission of the Southern states under Democratic control, for in that event, as Stevens never ceased reminding his colleagues, the former Confederates, "with their kindred Copperheads of the North, would always elect the President and control Congress."

This large Republican majority did not, however, work as a unit. Eight of these Congressmen were so independent in their views on Reconstruction legislation as to fall into no recognizable category. Such, for example, was Rufus P. Spalding, who was known at home as "the great Radical of Ohio" but whose course in the 1866–67 debates led him to consider himself "somewhat conservative." In general no faction of the party could depend upon the votes of these men during the critical preliminary stages when legislation was drafted and modified, though on a final vote they usually joined the other Republicans in a public, but meaningless, display of party unanimity.

Far more cohesive and positive were the thirty-two Republicans (with whom one dissident Democrat regularly voted) who formed the Moderate faction. Constantly aware of the need to conciliate the Democrats among their own constituents, they were loath to consider imposing drastic terms, such as Negro suffrage or confiscation of estates, upon the South. The best Republican policy, Moderate James H. Rice, of Maine, declared, was "to divide the people of the South in political sentiment, so that they will organize into antagonistic parties instead of consolidating into one party, [which will affiliate] . . . with the Democratic party of the North." At the same time the Moderate Republicans insisted that the Southerners must agree to protect the freedmen's civil rights. To most Moderates the Fourteenth Amendment —which, it will be remembered, made the Negroes citizens but allowed the Southern states themselves to choose between enfranchising the freedmen or having their congressional representation reduced—seemed an entirely adequate program of Reconstruction, and they frequently recalled that its moderation had greatly helped them in carrying their marginal districts.

After January, 1867, however, these Moderates began to feel their position to be increasingly untenable as Southern state after Southern state rejected the proposed amendment. When Stevens tauntingly pointed out this evidence of Southern recalcitrance, John A. Bingham, of Ohio, the most articulate spokesman of the Moderate group, could only reply weakly: "If they have all rejected it it does not follow that they will not all yet accept it." Some Moderates thought the Southern rebuff called for "a vigorous effort to carry a part of the southern States for the amendment by a direct appeal to the people." Others, like James G. Blaine, argued that the Southerners should pay the penalty for their reluctance by being obliged not merely to ratify the amendment but to accept "the superadded and indispensable prerequisite of manhood suffrage." Bingham himself urged the high-handed expedient of having Congress declare that the amendment was adopted when "ratified by three fourths of the organized and represented States"—i.e., by the states of the North and West—and thus impose it upon the Southerners without consulting them.

As the Moderates lost strength, the Radicals gained it, and by February, 1867, seventy-two Representatives could be identified with the left wing of the party. Though large, the group was not cohesive. Thirteen Congressmen can best be classified as Independent Radicals, who usually went along with the other members of the faction in desiring to overthrow the Johnson provisional governments in the South, in demanding more protection for Southern freedmen and loyalists, and in hoping for the emergence in these "wasted regions" of a society characterized by "small farms, thrifty tillage, free schools, closely-associated communities, social independence, respect for honest labor, and equality of political rights." Among these Independent Radicals were many Congressmen who had been repeatedly elected by enormous majorities—like William B. Washburn, of Massachusetts, and James K. Moorhead, of Pennsylvania—and whose seats were so secure that they had a certain freedom to exercise independent judgment: they were not, therefore, dependable allies. Their fellow Radicals could not count upon them to take a leading part in the debates, and they frequently abstained or dissented on critical test votes.

More homogenous and disciplined was the contingent of forty-seven Radicals who followed Stevens' lead. They favored extreme measures for reconstructing the South, but when these were in danger of defeat, they readily agreed to modifications or even substitutes. Stevens himself, far from being an imperious whip who lashed his fellow Republicans into mute obedience, proved to be a shrewd and adaptable parliamentary leader, repeatedly agreeing to soften some detail of his Reconstruction plan "if it is going to offend any brother." Sharply hostile to the Moderates, the Stevens Radicals had no hesitation in working in tandem with the Democrats to defeat proposals sponsored by Bingham and Blaine.

A group of twelve Representatives, who might be called the Ultra Radicals, was unwilling to engage in such parliamentary games and preferred to preserve their doctrinal purity even at the cost of defeat. Such a Congressman was James M. Ashley, of Ohio, who asked not merely for military rule and Negro suffrage in the South but also insisted that the old state lines be erased and that nonsegregated schools be set up in the former Confederacy. Not active in the debates, these Ultras suspiciously watched their fellow Radicals and warned them whenever they seemed about to stray from principles. Even the seventy-year-old Stevens himself was not exempt from their censure, for when he proposed a measure that seemed to imply an indirect and limited recognition of the provisional governments in the South, an Ultra leaped to his feet to declare himself "appalled at the temerity of this rash young gentleman from Pennsylvania."

Simple political arithmetic gives the best explanation of why a Congress so divided pursued the course it did on the 1867 Reconstruction Act. If fully mustered, Radical strength was not quite enough to pass a bill in the House of Representatives and was far from enough to override an anticipated presidential veto. On the other hand, had it been practicable, a coalition of all regularly attending Moderate, Conservative, and Democratic Representatives would barely have been able to pass a bill over united Radical opposition. Such a combination, however, was very unlikely, since, as we have seen, ideological differences between the Moderate and Radical Republicans were not vast, while loyalty to party was deeply ingrained. Few Republicans of any persuasion could withstand Stevens' taunt that by assenting to Democratic Reconstruction proposals they would be taking a "step toward universal Andy-Johnsonism" and would next be "hugging and caressing those whose hands are red and whose garments are dripping with the blood of our and their murdered kindred."

Given these facts, any new Reconstruction legislation passed during the second session of the Thirty-Ninth Congress was going to have to be a compromise, whose provisions were acceptable to a majority of all Republicans, whatever their faction. The legislative history of the 1867 Reconstruction Act is the story of the evolution of such a compromise. One might think of it as a tug of war between Republican factions, with the Democrats trying to perpetuate the contest by giving an occasional boost to whichever team seemed about to lose. Or it could be pictured as a seesaw, with numbers of small children of assorted weights, each representing a faction of the Democratic and Republican parties, trying to tip the balance one way or the other. But perhaps it would be easiest to conceive of the legislative process as a pendulum, which, once set in motion, vibrates in ever diminishing arcs until the bob comes to rest at dead center.

III

When Stevens introduced his drastic Reconstruction proposals on January 3, 1867, he gave the legislative pendulum a sharp pull to the left (see Figure IV). Seeking to take advantage of the momentum Stevens had imparted, the Ultra Radicals promptly attempted to force the pendulum further in the same direction. No sooner had Stevens made this proposal than Ashley moved a substitute, which called for the permanent disqualification of all Confederate civil and military officeholders, insisted upon "a well-organized system of free schools . . . from which no child shall be excluded because of race or color," and provided for the partition of Texas into two states.

Instantly, however, it was clear that in politics as in physics action produces reaction. Not only did the anticipated Democratic and Conservative opposition to these Radical proposals appear, but Bingham, leading the Moderate Republicans, vigorously attacked them and urged that they be referred to the Joint Committee on Reconstruction, where he knew they would be drastically altered or quietly buried.

For the next three weeks the debate raged in the House. Many of the dozens of speeches were set pieces, blasting the reign of license and terror alleged to prevail at the South under the Johnson regimes or warning of the hypothetical dangers of Negro rule, and often they seemed to have no

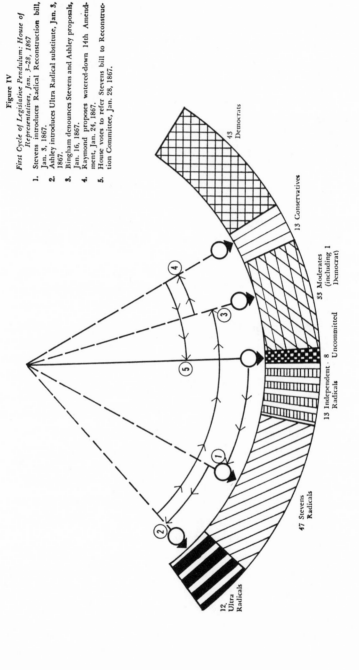

Figure IV

*First Cycle of Legislative Pendulum: House of
Representatives, Jan. 3–28, 1867*

1. Stevens introduces Radical Reconstruction bill,
   Jan. 3, 1867.
2. Ashley introduces Ultra Radical substitute, Jan. 3,
   1867.
3. Bingham denounces Stevens and Ashley proposals,
   Jan. 16, 1867.
4. Raymond proposes watered-down 14th Amendment, Jan. 24, 1867.
5. House votes to refer Stevens bill to Reconstruction Committee, Jan. 28, 1867.

43
Democrats

13 Conservatives

33 Moderates
(including 1
Democrat)

8
Uncommitted

13 Independent
Radicals

Independent
Radicals

47 Stevens
Radicals

12,
Ultra
Radicals

particular relevance either to the merits of the Stevens and Ashley proposals or to the desirability of Bingham's plan to refer them both to committee for further consideration. Behind the verbiage, however, one can sense that the legislative pendulum was slowly moving toward the right. Adroitly, using every parliamentary weapon in the book, Stevens fought to stop the swing. Alternatively he threatened and cajoled. He showed himself intractable and then conciliatory. The very desperateness of his maneuvers indicated his awareness that he could not rally a majority of the House behind any Radical measure. Originally he had hoped for a quick vote, but, sensing impending defeat, he secured on January 7 a one-week postponement of further debate. The delay did not strengthen his position. Seeking to appease the critics of his plan, he pledged on January 17 that, if Bingham's motion to recommit both Radical proposals was voted down, he would not invoke the previous question and cut off further debate but would give "an opportunity to any gentleman who may desire to offer amendments." On January 21 he called for an evening session, in the vain hope that the Congressmen would talk themselves out and he could secure a vote the next day. But, though Radicals in great numbers spoke for his plan, Stevens saw that he did not have the votes and was obliged to allow the debate to go on.

By this time the pendulum had swung as far right as Stevens and Ashley had originally pulled it to the left. Enemies of Stevens' proposal seemed no longer content with Bingham's plan quietly to kill it in committee. Moderates, Conservatives, and Democrats began to unite behind a plan, originally suggested by the Conservative Henry J. Raymond, to strip the proposed Fourteenth Amendment of its clause disqualifying ex-Confederates from office and to offer this revised version as the new basis for Reconstruction in the South.

Sensing the danger—and also doubtless sensing that the pendulum had swung too far to the right to suit most Moderate Republicans—Stevens on January 24 resorted to drastic tactics to reverse the trend. "If I do not change my mind," he warned the stunned Congressmen, "I shall to-morrow relieve the House from any question upon the merits of this bill by moving to lay it on the table." His announcement was a clear threat to the Radicals that, if they did not all rally behind him, they would end with no new Reconstruction legislation, but, more significantly, it was a warning to the Moderates that further collaboration with Democrats and Conservatives would break up the Republican party. Promptly the legislative pendulum reversed itself and began moving back toward the perpendicular.

Two days later Stevens sought to take advantage of the change in direction caused by his surprise move and asked both Ashley and Bingham to withdraw their motions. Ashley, for the Ultra Radicals, agreed, but the Moderates were still unwilling to have the pendulum come to rest at a point so far to the left as Stevens demanded. Stevens then sought to placate them by incorporating several of their minor proposed amendments in his bill, but Bingham was not content and refused to withdraw his motion referring the whole matter back to the Joint Committee. "I desire the House to decide . . . ," he declared, "whether we shall recede from the principles of the pending constitutional amendment to the extent to which this bill does as it now stands." Furious, Stevens warned "that the reference of the bill to . . . committee is the death of the measure." When Bingham dissented from this opinion "of the venerable gentleman from Pennsylvania," Stevens snarled: "The gentleman will recollect that I did not ask his concurrence. In all this contest about reconstruction I do not propose either to take his counsel, recognize his authority, or believe a word he says."

For all their anger, Stevens and his fellow Radicals realized they did not have a majority, and they sought once more to soften their proposal by substituting for Stevens' Draconian measure a milder version by Samuel Shellabarger, of Ohio, which would have caused only Confederates who had held rank above that of second lieutenant to forfeit citizenship.

Up to this point, though the legislative pendulum had swung wildly from left to right and back again toward center, there had been no voting on the proposed Reconstruction measure, for Stevens, aware of Radical weakness, had carefully refrained from demanding a roll call. Now, believing that he had all groups of Radicals behind him and that his concessions had won over some Moderates, he was ready to force the issue. Warning that there was only a very brief time during which Congress could pass this bill and then repass it over the President's veto, he demanded a vote on January 28. Democrats and Conservatives joined with the Moderates and five of the Independent Radicals to support Bingham's proposition (88–65) and referred Stevens' plan back to committee.

Thus the legislative pendulum again came to rest at dead center, just where it had been before the Christmas holidays. The debates had proved that neither the Ultra Radicals nor Stevens' regular following could have their way in revolutionizing the South; they had also proved that neither Bingham's hope of making the Moderate Fourteenth Amendment the final condition of restoration nor the Conservative wish to submit a watered-down version of that amendment could be adopted.

IV

The second cycle of the legislative pendulum began on February 2, 1867, when Stevens, finally admitting that non-Radical support was needed to pass any Reconstruction bill,

called the Joint Committee of Fifteen into session, for the
first time since June, 1866 (see Figure V). He was not able
to persuade the committee to accept his proposal, which the
House just voted to refer to that body, and the meeting
broke up inconclusively. When the committee met again,
four days later, there was a new plan of Reconstruction for
it to consider, the precise origins of which are not clear. As
early as January 19, the unpredictable Spalding of Ohio had
urged that the Southern states be "placed under martial
law for and during the whole period" before their readmission. More influential, however, was the voice of the Radical
George W. Julian, of Indiana, who spoke on the very day
Stevens' bill was recommitted. Objecting to any plan for
"the early restoration of the rebellious districts to their
former places in the Union," Julian proposed instead "that
Congress shall organize a well-appointed political *purgatory,*
located in the rebellious districts, and keep the rebels in it"
for perhaps "ten years, or twenty years." During this pro-
bationary period, he urged, there should be military government to make these states "safe for the freedmen of the South,
safe for her loyal white men, safe for the emigrants from the
Old World and from the northern States to go and dwell
there," so that, in time, there would emerge in the South
"a Christian civilization and a living democracy amid the
ruins of the past." On February 4 Senator George H. Williams, of Oregon, who had frequently acted with the Moderates in the past but had been drifting into the group of
Independent Radicals, introduced a bill accepting Julian's
idea and placing the ten unreconstructed states under martial
law, with a suspension of the privilege of the writ of habeas
corpus.

At its February 6 meeting the Joint Committee finally rejected Stevens' bill and, after minor amendments, endorsed
Williams' strictly military plan. Ironically enough, Stevens

Figure V

Second Cycle of Legislative Pendulum: House of Representatives, Jan. 28–Feb. 13, 1867

1. Stalemate in House as Moderates succeed in referring Stevens' Radical Reconstruction bill to committee, Jan. 28, 1867.
2. Stevens introduces new military Reconstruction bill, Feb. 6, 1867.
3. Bingham and Blaine propose amendments allowing restoration of Southern states, Feb. 12, 1867.
4. With Democratic help, Stevens defeats Blaine's motion to refer his military bill to committee and forces passage through House, Feb. 13, 1867.

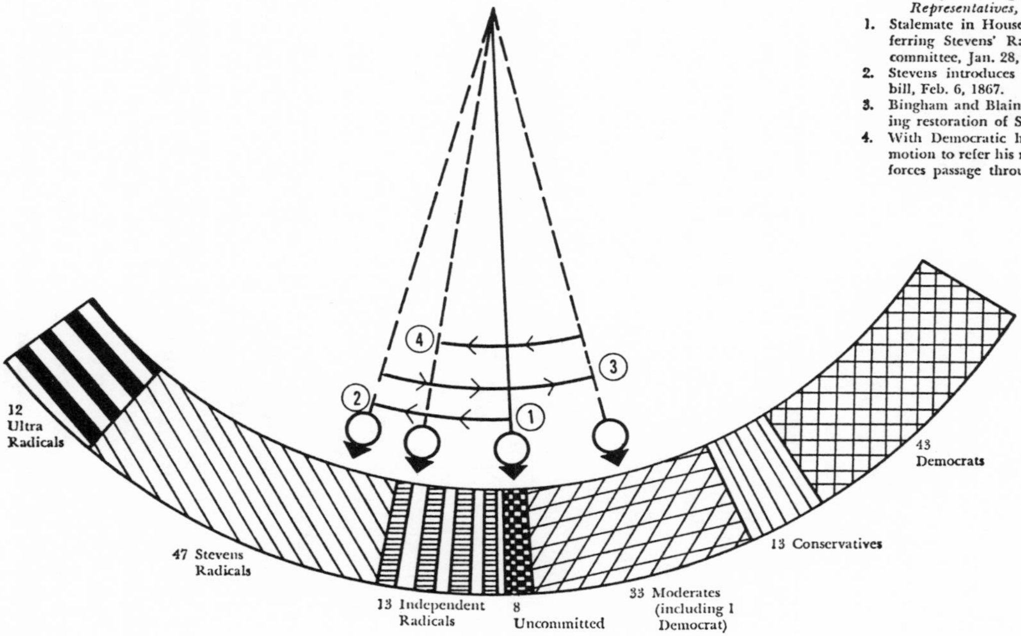

48 Democrats

13 Conservatives

33 Moderates (including 1 Democrat)

8 Uncommitted

13 Independent Radicals

47 Stevens Radicals

12 Ultra Radicals

himself was directed to report the military proposal to the
House. That Stevens was unhappy with the new bill is
evidenced by the fact that he called the Joint Committee into
session only one more time and, there being no quorum, adjourned it; thus it ignominiously died. But, whatever his
personal wishes, Stevens was the House Republican leader,
and in his eyes a military bill was better than no legislation
at all. Promptly on February 6 he again pulled the legislative
pendulum to the left—but not quite so far this time—introducing a brief bill dividing the recalcitrant states into five
military districts. The proposal set no time limit to this
military rule, and it set forth no conditions with which the
Southerners could comply and expect readmission. Defend-
ing the measure on the following day, Stevens frankly admitted that it was somewhat improvised because of the "difficulty in harmonizing the councils of the dominant party,"
but he declared it was necessary to prevent further "perse-
cution, exile, [and] murder" of loyalists in the South. The
House must act promptly because there were "now perhaps
less than fifteen days this side of a veto in which this bill must
pass this House and pass the Senate and be acted upon [by
the President], if it is to become a law." "To-morrow," he
pledged, "God willing, I will demand the vote."

Immediately the counterswing of the pendulum began, but
just as Stevens had not pulled so far to the left in beginning
this second cycle, so the swing to the right was not so marked.
For the Moderates Bingham declared his "hearty approval"
of the general purpose of the proposed bill, which was "in
perfect harmony with all the legislation of this Government
since the breaking out of the rebellion." He did, however,
urge amendments, especially a statement informing the
Southerners "what they have to do, and all they have to do,
in order to get rid of military rule and military government."
Four days later Bingham brought in some rather complex and

technical amendments which he thought would accomplish this end, and on the same day Blaine proposed to add to the military bill a simple statement that the Southern states could expect readmission after they ratified the Fourteenth Amendment and guaranteed impartial suffrage, "without regard to race, color, or previous condition of servitude, except [to] such as may be disfranchised for participating in the late rebellion."

In this second cycle of the legislative pendulum, the debates were often heated, but they lacked the factional ferocity which had marked the discussion of Stevens' original proposal. Most Radicals opposed any substantial amendment of the military bill. It was, they declared, a measure supported with unprecedented unanimity by the Republicans in the Joint Committee; any alteration would imperil party unity; there was not time to mature a comprehensive Reconstruction program, and, anyway, the bill which Radical Representative T. D. Eliot, of Massachusetts, introduced on February 11 for the reorganization of Louisiana would serve to indicate the steps Southerners would have to take before they would be welcome in Washington. Even so, most of the Radicals admitted that the military bill was only "a temporary measure," necessary "to guaranty present protection and equal justice to the Union men of the South." Moderates, on the other hand, acquiesced in military rule but deplored the failure of the military bill to give Southern whites any incentive to seek readmission. Though Stevens desponded over the "demoralization" of the House Republicans and doubted "if there is enough of the spirit of the party that sent us here to carry out the will of the people and perfect the legislation they expected from us," in all probability the House Republicans, left to themselves, would have reached some compromise between Stevens' purely military bill and the Moderate amendments setting forth conditions for the return of civilian rule in the South.

At this point, however, the Democrats deliberately prevented the pendulum from coming to rest. Hoping if possible to prolong the debates until the end of the session, when the President could kill any bill by a pocket veto, and eager to make the Republicans sponsor legislation as objectionable as possible to Southern whites, Democrats gave the pendulum a strong push to the left by attacking Bingham's "monomania of radicalism" and declaring that, if Reconstruction legislation must be passed, they preferred the plan sponsored by "the gentleman from Pennsylvania . . . because he is more open and undisguised."

With the pendulum again swinging in his direction, Stevens refused to make any but the most trivial concessions to the Moderates. On February 13 he invoked the authority of the Joint Committee to support his position. Though it had not met in many days and had never debated the proposed Moderate amendments, Stevens blandly told the House "that after full examination the committee think the bill cannot be made to suit them better and the country than it is; and the last one they would favor is the amendment of the gentleman from Maine [i.e., Blaine]."

The Moderates tried to counter the drift by having Bingham withdraw his complicated proposals and by agreeing upon Blaine's simple amendment, which, at the same time, he slightly modified so as to be more attractive to the Democrats. Then, feeling strong enough for a test, on February 13 Blaine moved to refer the whole bill, including the amendments, to the judiciary committee, which the Moderates controlled. With all his virtuoso powers Stevens fought Blaine's motion. He called attention to his "physical inability" in his declining years; he castigated "the supineness with which this Congress had conducted itself"; he engaged in harsh personalities, branding Bingham's conduct as "most unparliamentary and discourteous"; he said the Bingham-Blaine amendment would lead "this House, possibly by forbidden paths, into the sheepfold or the goatfold of the President"; he warned that the amendment, if adopted, would amount to "an entire surrender . . . into the hands of the rebels." When the vote was taken, however, it was evident that Stevens' eloquence had changed few opinions. To be sure, the House refused (94–69) to send the bill to committee, but Stevens' majority was made possible by the fact that twenty-three Democrats voted with him in an effort to keep the bill in Radical hands and make it as offensive as possible to the Moderates, to the President, and to the South.

Immediately thereafter, the House voted on Stevens' military bill as a whole. Since the Moderates had now no choice but to support it or to be content with no Reconstruction legislation, the measure was passed by a party vote (109–55), with only thirteen Conservatives in opposition. Gloatingly Stevens addressed the chair: " . . . I wish to inquire, Mr. Speaker, if it is in order for me now to say that we indorse the language of good old Laertes, that Heaven rules as yet and there are gods above?" Thus, apparently, the second cycle of the legislative pendulum had ended with a Radical victory.

V

Stevens' rejoicing was, however, premature, for equilibrium had not yet been reached, but the third cycle of the legislative pendulum was to take place in the Senate, which had up to this point been strangely silent on Reconstruction issues, pending the outcome of the House struggle (see Figure VI). Promptly now, however, on February 13, 1867, the Senate moved to take up both the Louisiana Reconstruction bill and the military Reconstruction bill. The ensuing de-

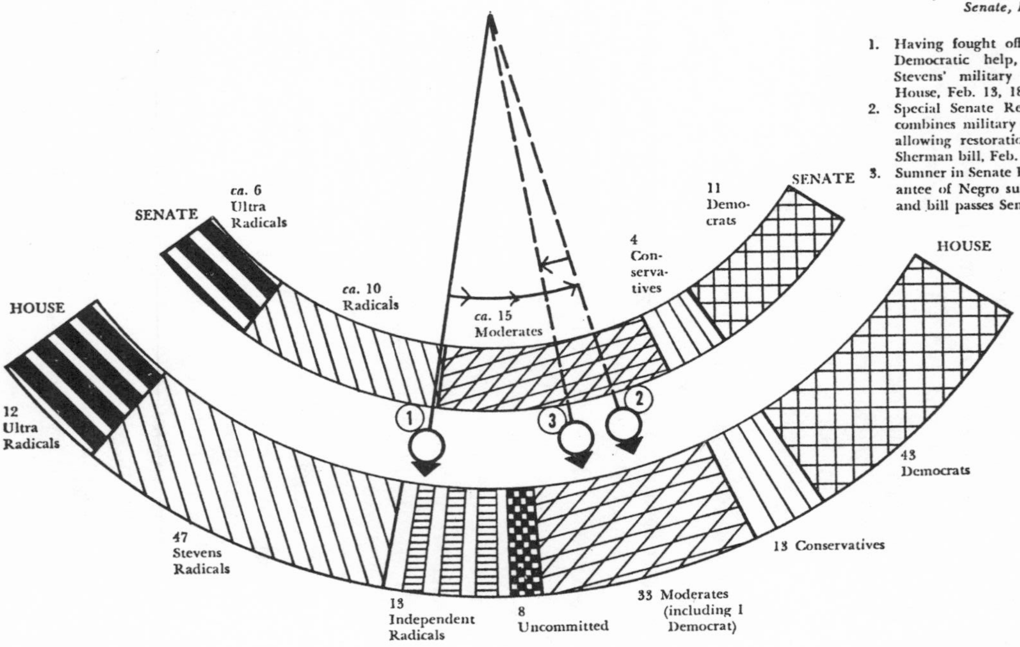

Figure VI

Third Cycle of Legislative Pendulum: House and Senate, Feb. 13-17, 1867

1. Having fought off Moderate amendments with Democratic help, Radicals force passage of Stevens' military Reconstruction bill through House, Feb. 13, 1867.

2. Special Senate Republican committee of seven combines military bill with Blaine's amendment allowing restoration of Southern states in new Sherman bill, Feb. 16, 1867.

3. Sumner in Senate Republican caucus secures guarantee of Negro suffrage in South, Feb. 16, 1867, and bill passes Senate, Feb. 17, 1867.

bates were necessarily briefer than those in the House, because of the deadline imposed by the anticipated presidential pocket veto, and they are not so revealing as in the House discussions, since most important factional differences were explored and settled in the secret Republican caucus, not on the Senate floor.

Senator Williams, who was in charge of the military Reconstruction bill, already passed by the House, hoped the Senate would adopt it quickly and without amendment, but his dream of Republican unanimity was shattered when Democratic Senator Reverdy Johnson promptly introduced an amendment virtually identical with that advocated by Blaine in the House. Immediately factional differences appeared among the Republican Senators. Senator William M. Stewart, of Nevada, approved Reverdy Johnson's proposal. "There must be a road of escape," he insisted, "or I cannot vote for this military bill." Simultaneously Radicals moved to make the bill more stringent. Henry Wilson, of Massachusetts, proposed an amendment guaranteeing all citizens in the South "the right to pursue all lawful avocations and business" and "to receive the equal benefits of the public schools." His Radical colleague, Sumner, declared that the failure of the military Reconstruction bill explicitly to outlaw the existing governments in the South, to guarantee Negro suffrage in all future elections, and to disfranchise many Confederates made it "so thoroughly vicious in every line and in every word from the first to the last that . . . it ought to be amended from the first word to the last."

Quickly the Republican Senate leaders decided to prevent further advertisement of their factional differences by entrusting the whole Reconstruction issue to a special committee of seven, with the Moderate John Sherman, of Ohio, as chairman. On Saturday morning, February 16, while two voluble Senators held the floor with rambling speeches, the committee met and agreed upon a measure which, except for a few verbal alterations, combined Stevens' military bill with Blaine's conditions for the readmission of the South. This Sherman bill—as it ought henceforth to be called— struck Sumner as being too Moderate, and in the Republican Senate caucus, which met Saturday afternoon, he was able to swing the pendulum back slightly to the left, securing by a two-vote majority agreement that Negro suffrage would be required not merely in the election of constitutional conventions in the South but in all subsequent elections held under the new state constitutions. The bill was then rushed to the Senate that same day and, after a prolonged evening session, it was passed at 6:22 A.M. on Sunday morning, by a strict party vote. By virtue of the Senate's action the pendulum had once again swung to the Moderate side, not quite so far as in previous cycles but far enough to insure that there would inevitably follow a counterswing when the amended measure was reviewed by House Radicals.

Promptly on Monday, February 18, the fourth cycle of the pendulum began when the House learned of the Senate action (see Figure VII). Furious, Stevens immediately moved that the House should not concur in the Senate amendments. "Pass this bill," he warned, "and you open the flood-gates of misery; you disgrace . . . the Congress of the United States." No appeals could move him. He was indifferent to Bingham's complaint that he was betraying the platform upon which many Republicans had triumphed at the recent election; he ignored Farnsworth's warning "that we must pass this bill or else pass no bill"; he scorned Garfield's challenge to "quote a line . . . or a single word from the bill itself," showing "that it does any one of the horrible things they tell us of."

Jubilantly the Democrats watched the Republican discord, and they contributed to it whenever possible by delivering long speeches, behaving boisterously, and making frequent

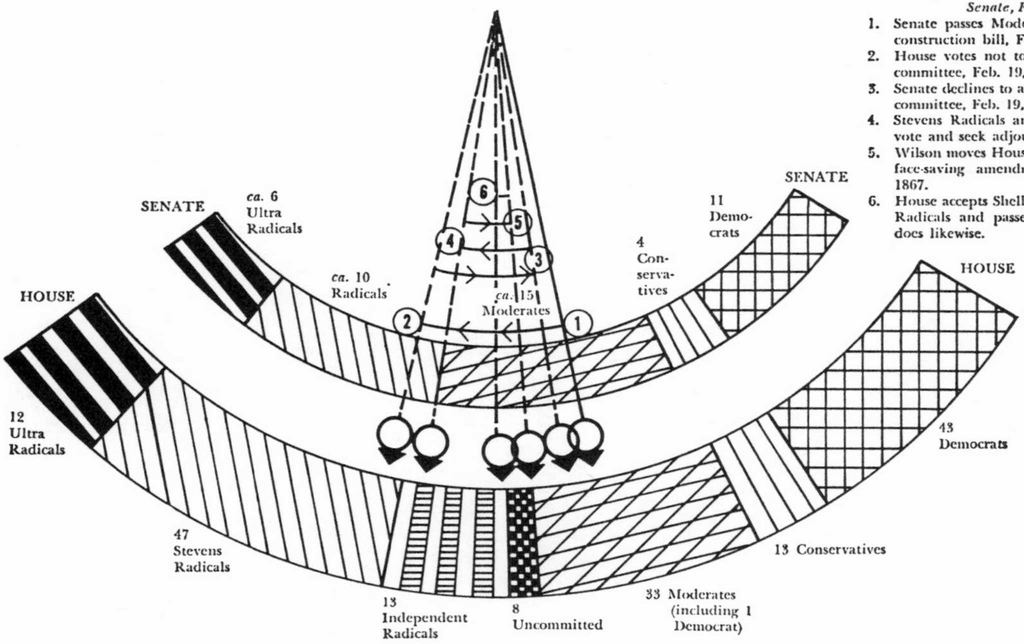

Figure VII

Final Cycles of Legislative Pendulum: House and Senate, Feb. 17–20, 1867

1. Senate passes Moderate Sherman version of Reconstruction bill, Feb. 17, 1867.
2. House votes not to concur, appoints conference committee, Feb. 19, 1867.
3. Senate declines to appoint members to conference committee, Feb. 19, 1867.
4. Stevens Radicals and Democrats in House delay vote and seek adjournment, Feb. 19, 1867.
5. Wilson moves House adoption of Senate bill with face-saving amendment for Radicals, Feb. 19, 1867.
6. House accepts Shellabarger's further concession to Radicals and passes bill, Feb. 20, 1867. **Senate does likewise.**

calls to order and motions to adjourn. On February 19 all but two of the Democrats voted, along with four-fifths of Stevens' personal following and three-fifths of the Ultra Radicals, not to concur in the Senate amendments.

But when the Senate learned of the House action, the pendulum again swung swiftly back to the right. Strongly disapproving of the coalition House Radicals had formed with the Democrats, Sherman led the Moderate Republicans of the Senate in refusing to recede from their amendments and in declining to go into conference over differences between the House and Senate versions of the bill.

When the Senate's intransigence was reported to House, the legislative pendulum made one final oscillation to the left. Stevens openly collaborated with Democratic dilatory motions designed to prevent House concurrence in the Senate bill and, though many of his followers now began to desert him, he still had enough strength on February 20 to defeat Blaine's motion to cut off further debate. At this point it appeared, just as it had appeared at the beginning of the session and on January 28, when the House referred Stevens' original proposal back to committee, that the Republican factions in the Thirty-Ninth Congress could agree on no Reconstruction legislation.

To prevent total stalemate, the Independent Radical James F. Wilson, of Iowa, proposed a compromise. Agreeing to the Senate version of the Reconstruction bill—the Sherman bill, which it will be remembered, was a marriage of Stevens' original military bill with Blaine's amendment setting forth conditions of restoration—Wilson asked, however, for the Radicals a face-saving concession in the form of an amendment which would exclude anybody from voting for or participating in the Southern constitutional conventions who was disqualified under the terms of the proposed Fourteenth Amendment. Since this was still not quite enough to sugarcoat the pill for Stevens and his followers, who once more voted to let the debate run on, Samuel Shellabarger attempted to win one slight additional concession for the Radicals by adding a further amendment that made explicit the power of the federal government "at any time to abolish, modify, control, or supersede" the existing provisional regimes in the South.

This was too much for many Moderates, who joined the Democrats in voting against yielding so much to the Radicals, but eighteen Moderates joined the three almost unanimous Radical groups in backing Shellabarger's plan, and it was adopted, as was Wilson's amendment. With these two changes, to which the Senate promptly assented, the law was finally passed by both houses on February 20 and was sent to the President.

On March 2 President Johnson returned the unsigned bill with the expected veto message. With almost no discussion, both houses, by overwhelming votes (38–10 in the Senate, 135–48 in the House), promptly repassed the bill, and the pattern which shaped the political, economic, and social development of the South for the next decade was set.

One of the most far-reaching and influential measures ever passed by an American Congress, the Reconstruction Act of 1867 was not the work of any man or of any faction. Democrats and Radical Republicans alike were responsible for its provisions, and Moderate Republicans and Conservatives also helped shape its outlines. Republicans as diverse as James M. Ashley, Thaddeus Stevens, John A. Bingham, and Henry J. Raymond all opposed it at one stage or another, as, of course, did all varieties of Democrats. Nor can the act be understood as the product of a particular ideology. The vote of the Congressman who thought it too strong and that of the Congressman who thought it too weak were determined less by abstract ideas than by the degree of strength and security each felt in his home district. The legislative history of the bill is the story of a series of attempted compromises between the need of the individual Congressman to respond to the desires of his constituency and the necessity for the national Republican party to enact a comprehensive Reconstruction program. The process by which Congress came to pass this legislation can best be described in quasi-mechanical terms as an equilibrium achieved by a resolution of quantitatively measurable forces.

At the outset of this book, I suggested that the historiography of the Reconstruction period has nearly reached a stalemate because of the difficulty of fathoming the motives of the leading actors and because of the impossibility of agreeing upon standards by which their actions should be valued. In these three essays I have tried to suggest that there may be other roads, by-passing these traditional, snarled questions, which can profitably be explored. In concentrating upon impersonal forces and patterns of behavior in these essays, it is not my purpose to argue that consideration of moral judgments and motivations should, once and for all, be excluded from history. Instead, I have simply directed myself to the task of devising a new strategy for attacking a problem where more conventional approaches have proved less than successful. The methods here suggested should not be taken to be intrinsically valuable unless, when developed by other scholars, they will help create a new synthesis on the Reconstruction period which can embrace both the unique and the representative, take into account both the mixed motives of individuals and the mixed moral consequence of their actions, and integrate biographical studies of character and sociological studies of culture. Only such a synthesis can do justice to this most difficult and fascinating period in our history.

Voting Record
of Republican (or Union)
Representatives in 38th Congress (1864–65)
on Six Roll Calls

The six roll calls here tabulated are:

(1) On a proposal to add a preamble to the Davis Reconstruction bill declaring that the Confederates had "no right to claim the mitigation of the extreme rights of war" and announcing that none of the states of the Confederacy could "be considered and treated as entitled to be represented in Congress, or to take any part in the political government of the Union." The motion was defeated, May 4, 1864, by a vote of 57 to 76. Radical votes ("O") favored the proposal; Moderate votes ("X") opposed. (*Congressional Globe*, 38th Cong., 1st Sess., pp. 2107–08.)

(2) On a motion to remove a bill for the reconstruction of Louisiana from the House judiciary committee and give it to the special committee on the rebellious states. The vote, on December 13, 1864, was a tie (66–66), which the Speaker broke and defeated the motion. Radical votes ("O") favored the motion; Moderate votes ("X") opposed it. (*Ibid.*, 38th Cong., 2d Sess., p. 26.)

(3)   On a motion to postpone for two weeks further discussion
       of the bill for the reconstruction of Louisiana and other
       states. The motion was carried (103–34) on January 17,
       1865. Radical votes ("O") opposed; Moderate votes
       ("X") favored. (*Ibid.*, p. 301.)

(4)   On a motion to table this Reconstruction bill. The motion
       was carried (91–64), on February 21, 1865, with Radical
       votes ("O") opposing and many Moderate votes ("X")
       in favor of tabling. (*Ibid.*, pp. 970–71.)

(5)   On a motion to table the proposed reconsideration of the
       Reconstruction bill. The motion carried (92–57), on
       February 21, 1865. Radical votes ("O") opposed the
       motion; Moderate votes ("X") favored it. (*Ibid.*, p. 971.)

(6)   On a motion to table a bill providing that constitutional
       conventions in the Confederate states should be elected
       by loyal whites and Negroes who had served in the Union
       armies, to the exclusion of rebels. The motion was carried
       (80–65), on February 22, 1865. Radicals ("O") opposed
       the tabling, while Moderates ("X") favored it. (*Ibid.*,
       pp. 1002–03.)

Throughout the following tabulation, "A" indicates that the
member did not vote, whether because he was absent, because
he abstained, or because (in a very few cases) his right to a seat
had not yet been certified.

Voting percentages have been calculated from figures given in
The Tribune Almanac. Most states held congressional elections
in 1862, but a few elected Representatives in 1863. "N. a."
indicates that no statistics are available.

Representative	State	Percentage of Vote 1862 or 1863	Vote on Roll Calls					
			1	2	3	4	5	6
Alley, J. B.	Mass.	61.1	O	O	X	A	A	A
Allison, W. B.	Iowa	58.8	O	O	O	O	O	O
Ames, Oakes	Mass.	61.1	O	O	X	O	O	O
Anderson, Lucien	Ky.	85.4	O	A	A	X	X	X
Arnold, I. N.	Ill.	54.8	X	A	X	O	O	A
Ashley, J. M.	Ohio	38.5	O	X	O	O	O	O
Bailey, Joseph	Penn.	55.1	A	A	X	X	X	X
Baldwin, J. D.	Mass.	66.1	O	O	O	O	O	O
Baxter, Portus	Vt.	73.0	O	O	X	O	O	O
Beaman, F. C.	Mich.	50.3	O	X	O	O	O	O
Blaine, J. G.	Me.	60.3	A	O	X	O	O	A
Blair, J. B.	W.Va.	93.0	X	O	A	O	A	X
Blow, H. T.	Mo.	69.5	X	X	A	O	O	O
Boutwell, G. S.	Mass.	55.1	O	O	O	O	O	O
Boyd, S. H.	Mo.	62.5	O	O	X	X	X	O
Brandegee, Augustus	Conn.	58.1	A	A	O	O	O	O
Broomall, J. M.	Penn.	60.5	O	X	O	O	O	O
Clark, A. W.	N.Y.	57.3	A	O	X	O	O	O
Clarke, Freeman	N.Y.	53.2	A	O	X	A	A	A
Cobb, Amasa	Wisc.	56.3	A	O	X	X	X	X
Cole, Cornelius	Calif.	n.a.	O	O	X	O	O	O
Colfax, Schuyler	Ind.	50.3	Speaker					
Cresswell, J. A. J.	Md.	55.1	X	A	O	A	A	A
Davis, H. W.	Md.	99.6	O	X	O	O	O	O
Davis, T. T.	N.Y.	58.4	A	A	X	X	X	A
Dawes, H. L.	Mass.	56.2	A	O	X	X	X	X
Deming, H. C.	Conn.	50.8	A	O	X	O	O	O
Dixon, N. F.	R.I.	56.9	A	O	X	O	O	O
Donnelly, Ignatius	Minn.	58.5	O	O	X	O	O	O
Driggs, J. F.	Mich.	51.7	O	A	X	O	O	O
Dumont, Ebenezer	Ind.	53.3	A	A	A	O	O	O

Representative	State	Percent- age of Vote 1862 or 1863	Vote on Roll Calls					
			1	2	3	4	5	6
Eckley, E. R.	Ohio	52.4	O	O	X	X	X	O
Eliot, T. D.	Mass.	75.2	O	O	X	O	O	O
Farnsworth, J. F.	Ill.	72.4	X	O	X	O	X	A
Fenton, R. E.	N.Y.	63.1	X	A	resigned			
Frank, Augustus	N.Y.	52.0	O	A	X	A	A	A
Garfield, J. A.	Ohio	66.2	O	O	O	O	O	O
Gooch, D. W.	Mass.	56.9	A	O	A	X	X	X
Grinnell, J. B.	Iowa	52.8	O	O	O	O	O	O
Higby, William	Calif.	n.a.	O	O	X	O	O	O
Hooper, Samuel	Mass.	52.2	O	O	A	O	O	O
Hotchkiss, G. W.	N.Y.	58.6	O	A	A	A	A	A
Hubbard, A. W.	Iowa	66.1	O	O	X	O	A	O
Hubbard, J. H.	Conn.	50.8	O	O	X	O	O	O
Hulburd, C. T.	N.Y.	67.1	X	O	A	X	X	O
Ingersoll, E. C.	Ill.	n.a.	A	O	X	O	X	O
Jenckes, T. A.	R.I.	58.5	A	O	A	O	A	O
Julian, G. W.	Ind.	55.5	O	X	A	X	X	A
Kasson, J. A.	Iowa	58.3	O	O	O	A	A	X
Kelley, W. D.	Penn.	52.4	O	O	O	O	O	O
Kellogg, F. W.	Mich.	57.8	O	O	O	O	O	A
Kellogg, Orlando	N.Y.	52.2	X	A	X	O	O	O
Knox, S. T.	Mo.	41.2	A	O	O	O	O	O
Littlejohn, D. C.	N.Y.	59.9	O	A	X	X	X	O
Loan, B. F.	Mo.	43.5	O	O	A	O	O	O
Longyear, J. W.	Mich.	51.7	O	X	O	O	O	O
Marvin, J. M.	N.Y.	51.0	X	O	X	X	X	X
McBride, J. R.	Ore.	65.2	O	O	O	O	O	O
McClurg, J. W.	Mo.	53.2	O	O	O	O	O	O
McIndoe, W. D.	Wisc.	58.1	X	O	X	A	A	A
Miller, S. F.	N.Y.	52.4	A	X	X	O	O	O
Moorhead, J. K.	Penn.	58.6	O	O	A	O	O	O

Representative	State	Percent-age of Vote 1862 or 1863	Vote on Roll Calls					
			1	2	3	4	5	6
Morrill, J. S.	Vt.	70.3	X	O	X	O	O	O
Morris, Daniel	N.Y.	58.7	O	O	O	O	O	O
Myers, Amos	Penn.	51.7	O	O	X	O	O	O
Myers, Leonard	Penn.	50.1	O	O	X	O	O	O
Norton, J. O.	Ill.	55.7	O	A	X	O	X	A
O'Neill, Charles	Penn.	58.6	O	O	X	O	O	O
Orth, G. S.	Ind.	51.8	O	O	X	O	O	O
Patterson, J. W.	N.H.	50.6	O	O	X	O	A	A
Perham, Sidney	Me.	56.9	O	O	X	O	O	O
Pike, F. A.	Me.	52.7	O	O	X	X	X	X
Pomeroy, T. M.	N.Y.	55.2	X	X	A	X	X	X
Price, Hiram	Iowa	58.1	O	O	X	O	O	O
Randall, W. H.	Ky.	97.5	X	O	X	X	X	X
Rice, A. H.	Mass.	50.1	X	O	X	X	X	X
Rice, J. H.	Me.	60.6	O	O	X	O	O	O
Rollins, E. H.	N.H.	50.8	O	O	X	O	O	O
Schenck, R. C.	Ohio	52.5	O	X	O	O	O	O
Scofield, Glenni	Penn.	51.2	X	O	O	O	O	O
Shannon, T. B.	Calif.	n.a.	O	O	X	O	O	O
Sloan, I. C.	Wisc.	54.6	O	X	O	O	O	O
Smithers, N. B.	Del.	99.9	X	X	O	O	O	O
Spalding, R. P.	Ohio	68.8	O	O	X	A	A	A
Starr, J. F.	N.J.	51.4	A	X	O	O	O	O
Stevens, Thaddeus	Penn.	62.5	O	X	X	X	X	O
Thayer, M. R.	Penn.	50.1	X	A	X	O	O	O
Thomas, Francis	Md.	100.0	A	A	X	X	X	A
Tracy, H. W.	Penn.	55.2	A	O	A	X	X	X
Upson, Charles	Mich.	55.4	O	O	O	O	O	O
Van Valkenburg, R. B.	N.Y.	57.9	A	O	X	X	X	O
Washburn, W. B.	Mass.	100.0	O	O	X	X	X	X
Washburne, E. B.	Ill.	60.7	A	O	X	A	A	O

Representative	State	Percentage of Vote 1862 or 1863	Vote on Roll Calls					
			1	2	3	4	5	6
Webster, E. H.	Md.	100.0	X	A	X	X	X	A
Wilder, A. C.	Kans.	63.3	O	X	O	A	A	O
Williams, Thomas	Penn.	54.0	O	X	X	O	O	O
Wilson, J. F.	Iowa	54.7	X	O	X	O	O	O
Windom, William	Minn.	57.4	X	O	A	A	A	A
Woodbridge, F. E.	Vt.	71.0	O	A	A	O	A	O
Worthington, H. G.	Nev.	n.a.	A	A	X	O	O	A

II

Representatives
Who Voted Radical on 1864–65
Roll Calls

Group A. *Representatives who voted Radical on all six roll calls:*

Allison, W. B. (Iowa)
Baldwin, J. D. (Mass.)
Boutwell, G. S. (Mass.)
Garfield, J. A. (Ohio)
Grinnell, J. B. (Iowa)
Kelley, W. D. (Penn.)
McBride, J. R. (Ore.)
McClurg, J. W. (Mo.)
Morris, Daniel (N. Y.)
Upson, Charles (Mich.)

Group B. *Representatives who showed one deviation from Radical pattern:*

Ames, Oakes (Mass.)
Ashley, J. M. (Ohio)
Baxter, Portus (Vt.)
Beaman, F. C. (Mich.)
Broomall, J. M. (Penn.)

Cole, Cornelius (Calif.)
Davis, H. W. (Md.)
Donnelly, Ignatius (Minn.)
Eliot, T. D. (Mass.)
Higby, William (Calif.)
Hooper, Samuel (Mass.) (absent from one roll call)
Hubbard, J. H. (Conn.)
Kellogg, F. W. (Mich.) (absent from one roll call)
Knox, S. T. (Mo.) (absent from one roll call)
Loan, B. F. (Mo.) (absent from one roll call)
Longyear, J. W. (Mich.)
Moorhead, J. K. (Penn.) (absent from one roll call)
Myers, Amos (Penn.)
Myers, Leonard (Penn.)
O'Neill, Charles (Penn.)
Orth, G. S. (Ind.)
Perham, Sidney (Me.)
Price, Hiram (Iowa)
Rice, J. H. (Me.)
Rollins, E. H. (N.H.)
Schenck, R. C. (Ohio)
Scofield, Glenni (Penn.)
Shannon, T. B. (Calif.)
Sloan, I. C. (Wisc.)

Group C. *Representatives who showed two deviations from Radical pattern:*

Brandegee, Augustus (Conn.) (absent from two roll calls)
Clark, A. W. (N.Y.) (absent from one roll call)
Deming, H. C. (Conn.)
Dixon, N. F. (R.I.) (absent from one role call)
Driggs, J. F. (Mich.) (absent from one roll call)
Hubbard, A. W. (Iowa) (absent from one roll call)
Morrill, J. S. (Vt.)
Smithers, N. B. (Del.)
Starr, J. F. (N.J.) (absent from one roll call)
Williams, Thomas (Penn.)
Wilson, J. F. (Iowa)

III

Voting Record
of House of Representatives on
Reconstruction Measures During 2nd Session
of 39th Congress (1866–67)

Party affiliations of Congressmen during the Civil War-Reconstruction period are not always easy to ascertain or classify. Especially in the Border States a number of candidates ran as "Independents," "Unionists," "Constitutional Unionists," "Emancipationists," etc. Furthermore, some Representatives elected in 1864 as Republicans followed President Andrew Johnson in drifting into the Democratic party. The identification here is, therefore, in some cases only approximate. "R." stands for Republican; "D." for Democrat.

The first six of the roll-call votes here tabulated were used in determining membership of the factions of the Republican party. These six roll calls concern the following:

(1) The motion offered by John M. Broomall, of Pennsylvania, requiring the House committee on territories to look into the expediency of reporting a bill to establish territorial governments, with universal manhood suffrage, in all the former Confederate states except Tennessee. It passed (107–37) on December 4, 1866. Yea votes are indicated by

"O"; nays by "X." (*Congressional Globe*, 39th Cong., 2d Sess., p. 11.)

(2)   John A. Bingham's motion to refer the Reconstruction bill advocated by Thaddeus Stevens back to the Joint Committee of Fifteen on Reconstruction. The motion was carried (88–65), on January 28, 1867. Yea votes are indicated by "X"; nays by "O." (*Ibid.*, p. 817.)

(3)   The motion to order the main question on T. D. Eliot's bill to provide for the reconstruction of Louisiana. The main question was ordered (84–59) on February 11, 1867. Yea votes are indicated by "O"; nays by "X." (*Ibid.*, p. 1133.)

(4)   The motion to order the main question on J. G. Blaine's proposal to send the military Reconstruction bill to the House committee on the judiciary with instructions to report it with amendments. The main question was ordered (85–78) on February 13, 1867. Yea votes are indicated by "O"; nays by "X." (*Ibid.*, p. 1213.)

(5)   The motion of J. G. Blaine itself, just described. The motion was defeated (69–94), on February 13, 1867. Yea votes are indicated by "X"; nays by "O." (*Ibid.*, p. 1215.)

(6)   Stevens' motion to adopt the amended version of his military Reconstruction bill. The measure was passed (109–55) on February 13, 1867. Yea votes are indicated by "O"; nays by "X." (*Ibid.*, p. 1215.)

Four other votes, studied in conjunction with the previous six, are helpful in tracing the oscillations of the legislative pendulum on the 1867 Reconstruction Act:

(7)   The vote on R. P. Spalding's motion that the House concur in the amendments the Senate had made in the military Reconstruction bill. The motion was defeated (73–98), on February 19, 1867. Yea votes are indicated by "X"; nays by "O." (*Ibid.*, p. 1340.)

(8)   The vote on adjourning the House (thereby stalling further consideration of the Senate amendments) on February 19, 1867. The motion to adjourn lost (63–79). Yea votes are indicated by "O"; nays by "X." (*Ibid.*, p. 1357.)

(9) The vote on Samuel Shellabarger's amendment to the motion of J. F. Wilson that the House agree to the Senate amendments. Shellabarger's proposal affirmed the right of Congress to overthrow the provisional Johnson governments in the South. It was adopted (99–70) on February 20, 1867. Yea votes are indicated by "O"; nays by "X." (*Ibid.*, p. 1399.)

(10) The vote on the final passage of the amended Reconstruction Act. The bill carried (126–46) on February 20, 1867. Yea votes are indicated by "O"; nays by "X." (*Ibid.*, p. 1400.)

Throughout the following tabulation "A" indicates that the member did not vote, whether because he was absent, because he abstained, or because (in a very few cases) his right to a seat had not yet been certified. Votes set in italics are those of paired Congressmen, who, however, publicly indicated the side they would have supported if free to vote.

Vote on Roll Calls

Representative	State	Party	1	2	3	4	5	6	7	8	9	1(
Alley, J. B.	Mass.	R.	O	A	O	X	O	A	X	O	O	O
Allison, W. B.	Iowa	R.	O	O	O	O	X	O	X	X	O	O
Ames, Oakes	Mass.	R.	O	A	A	A	A	A	X	X	O	O
Ancona, S. E.	Penn.	D.	X	X	X	O	O	X	O	O	X	X
Anderson, G. W.	Mo.	R.	O	O	A	O	X	O	X	O	O	O
Arnell, S. M.	Tenn.	R.	O	A	O	X	O	O	O	X	O	O
Ashley, D. R.	Nev.	R.	A	X	A	O	X	O	X	X	O	O
Ashley, J. M.	Ohio	R.	O	O	O	O	O	O	O	O	O	O
Baker, Jehu	Ill.	R.	X	X	X	O	X	X	X	X	O	O
Baldwin, J. D.	Mass.	R.	O	O	O	O	X	A	X	X	O	O
Banks, N. P.	Mass.	R.	O	X	O	O	A	X	O	X	O	O
Barker, A. A.	Penn.	R.	O	O	O	X	O	O	X	X	X	O
Baxter, Portus	Vt.	R.	A	O	O	A	A	O	O	O	O	O
Beaman, F. C.	Mich.	R.	O	O	O	X	O	O	O	O	O	O
Benjamin, J. F.	Mo.	R.	A	A	A	A	X	O	X	A	X	O
Bergen, T. G.	N.Y.	D.	X	A	A	O	O	X	O	O	X	X
Bidwell, John	Calif.	R.	O	O	A	O	O	O	X	A	O	O
Bingham, J. A.	Ohio	R.	O	X	X	O	X	O	X	X	X	O
Blaine, J. G.	Me.	R.	A	X	O	O	X	O	X	X	X	O
Blow, H. T.	Mo.	R.	O	A	O	O	X	A	X	X	X	O
Boutwell, G. S.	Mass.	R.	O	O	O	X	O	O	O	O	O	O
Boyer, B. M.	Penn.	D.	X	X	X	O	O	X	O	O	X	X
Brandegee, Augustus	Conn.	R.	O	A	A	A	A	A	O	O	O	O
Bromwell, H. P. H.	Ill.	R.	O	A	A	X	O	O	O	X	O	O
Broomall, J. M.	Penn.	R.	O	O	O	O	X	O	O	X	O	O
Buckland, R. P.	Ohio	R.	O	X	A	O	X	O	X	X	X	O
Bundy, H. S.	Ohio	R.	O	X	A	O	X	O	X	A	O	O
Campbell, W. B.	Tenn.	D.	X	X	X	O	X	X	O	O	X	X
Chanler, J. W.	N.Y.	D.	X	X	X	X	O	X	O	A	X	X
Clarke, R. W.	Ohio	R.	O	O	O	O	O	O	X	O	O	O
Clarke, Sidney	Kans.	R.	O	A	O	X	O	O	O	A	O	O
Cobb, Amasa	Wisc.	R.	O	O	O	X	O	O	O	X	O	O
Colfax, Schuyler	Ind.	R.				Speaker						
Conkling, Roscoe	N.Y.	R.	A	X	A	A	A	A	A	A	A	A
Cook, B. C.	Ill.	R.	O	O	O	O	O	O	X	X	O	O

Vote on Roll Calls

Representative	State	Party	1	2	3	4	5	6		7	8	9	10
Cooper, Edmund	Tenn.	D.	A	X	X	O	X	X		O	O	X	X
Cullom, S. M.	Ill.	R.	O	O	O	X	O	O		X	A	O	O
Culver, C. V.	Penn.	R.	A	A	A	A	A	A		A	A	A	A
Darling, W. A.	N.Y.	R.	O	X	A	O	X	O		X	X	X	O
Davis, T. T.	N.Y.	R.	A	A	X	O	X	X		X	O	X	O
Dawes, H. L.	Mass.	R.	A	X	X	O	X	O		X	O	X	O
Dawson, J. L.	Penn.	D.	X	X	A	X	A	X		O	O	X	X
Defrees, J. H.	Ind.	R.	O	X	A	O	X	X		X	X	O	O
Delano, Columbus	Ohio	R.	A	X	A	O	X	O		X	X	X	O
Deming, H. C.	Conn.	R.	O	X	O	O	X	O		X	X	O	O
Denison, Charles	Penn.	D.	A	X	X	X	O	X		O	A	X	X
Dixon, N. F.	R.I.	R.	O	A	O	O	O	O		A	A	A	A
Dodge, W. E.	N.Y.	R.	X	X	X	O	X	X		X	X	X	O
Donnelly, Ignatius	Minn.	R.	A	O	O	O	O	O		O	O	O	O
Driggs, J. F.	Mich.	R.	O	O	A	X	O	O		O	A	A	A
Dumont, Ebenezer	Ind.	R.	A	A	O	O	O	O		O	A	O	O
Eckley, E. R.	Ohio	R.	O	O	O	X	O	O		X	A	A	A
Eggleston, Benjamin	Ohio	R.	O	X	O	O	O	O		X	X	O	O
Eldridge, Charles	Wisc.	D.	X	X	X	X	O	X		O	O	X	X
Eliot, T. D.	Mass.	R.	O	O	O	X	O	O		O	A	O	O
Farnsworth, J. F.	Ill.	R.	O	X	X	O	O	O		X	A	O	O
Farquhar, J. H.	Ind.	R.	O	X	O	O	O	O		O	X	O	O
Ferry, T. W.	Mich.	R.	O	X	O	A	X	O		X	A	O	O
Finck, W. E.	Ohio	D.	X	X	X	X	O	X		O	O	X	X
Garfield, J. A.	Ohio	R.	O	X	A	O	X	O		A	A	A	A
Glossbrenner, A. J.	Penn.	D.	X	A	X	X	O	X		A	O	X	X
Goodyear, Charles	N.Y.	D.	X	A	X	O	X	X		O	A	X	X
Grinnell, J. B.	Iowa	R.	O	O	O	X	O	O		O	X	O	O
Griswold, J. A.	N.Y.	R.	O	X	A	A	A	A		X	X	O	O
Hale, R. S.	N.Y.	R.	X	X	A	A	A	A		A	A	A	A
Harding, Aaron	Ky.	D.	A	X	X	X	O	X		O	O	X	X
Harding, Abner C.	Ill.	R.	O	O	A	X	O	O		O	X	O	O
Harris, B. G.	Md.	D.	A	X	A	X	O	X		O	A	A	A
Hart, Roswell	N.Y.	R.	O	O	A	A	A	A		X	X	O	O
Hawkins, I. R.	Tenn.	D.	O	X	X	A	X	X		O	O	A	X

Vote on Roll Calls

Representative	State	Party	1	2	3	4	5	6	7	8	9	10
Hayes, R. B.	Ohio	R.	O	O	O	O	O	O	O	X	O	O
Henderson, J. H. D.	Ore.	R.	O	A	O	X	O	O	O	X	O	O
Higby, William	Calif.	R.	O	O	O	X	O	O	O	O	O	O
Hill, Ralph	Ind.	R.	O	X	O	O	X	O	X	X	O	O
Hise, Elijah	Ky.	D.	A	X	X	A	X	X	O	O	X	X
Hogan, John	Mo.	D.	A	X	X	O	A	X	O	X	A	A
Holmes, S. T.	N.Y.	R.	O	O	O	X	O	O	O	O	O	O
Hooper, Samuel	Mass.	R.	O	X	O	X	O	O	X	A	O	O
Hotchkiss, G. W.	N.Y.	R.	A	O	O	A	A	A	O	O	O	O
Hubbard, A. W.	Iowa	R.	A	A	A	A	A	A	A	A	A	A
Hubbard, C. D.	W.Va.	R.	X	X	A	O	X	O	X	X	X	O
Hubbard, Demas, Jr.	N.Y.	R.	A	O	A	A	A	A	O	O	O	O
Hubbard, J. H.	Conn.	R.	O	O	O	X	O	O	O	A	O	O
Hubbell, E. N.	N.Y.	D.	A	X	X	O	X	X	O	A	X	X
Hubbell, J. R.	Ohio	R.	O	A	X	O	X	O	X	X	X	X
Hulburd, C. T.	N.Y.	R.	A	A	O	X	X	O	X	O	O	O
Humphrey, J. M.	N.Y.	D.	A	X	X	X	O	X	O	O	X	X
Hunter, J. W.	N.Y.	D.	X	A	X	X	X	X	O	O	X	X
Ingersoll, E. C.	Ill.	R.	O	X	O	X	O	O	O	A	O	O
Jenckes, T. A.	R.I.	R.	O	X	A	O	X	A	A	A	A	A
Johnson, Philip	Penn.	D.	A	A	died 29 Jan., 1867							
Jones, Morgan	N.Y.	D.	A	A	A	A	A	A	A	A	A	A
Julian, G. W.	Ind.	R.	O	O	O	X	O	A	O	X	O	O
Kasson, J. A.	Iowa	R.	O	O	A	A	A	A	X	X	A	O
Kelley, W. D.	Penn.	R.	O	O	O	X	O	O	O	X	O	O
Kelso, J. R.	Mo.	R.	A	A	A	O	X	X	O	O	O	O
Kerr, M. C.	Ind.	D.	X	A	X	O	O	X	O	O	X	X
Ketcham, J. H.	N.Y.	R.	A	X	A	O	X	O	X	X	O	O
Koontz, W. H.	Penn.	R.	O	O	O	X	O	O	O	A	O	O
Kuykendall, A. J.	Ill.	R.	X	X	X	O	X	X	O	O	X	X
Laflin, A. H.	N.Y.	R.	O	X	X	O	X	O	X	X	X	O
Latham, G. R.	W.Va.	D.	X	A	X	A	A	X	O	O	A	A
Lawrence, G. V.	Penn.	R.	O	X	O	O	X	O	X	X	X	O
Lawrence, William	Ohio	R.	O	A	O	O	X	O	X	X	O	O
LeBlond, F. C.	Ohio	D.	X	X	X	X	O	X	O	O	X	X

Vote on Roll Calls

Representative	State	Party	1	2	3	4	5	6		7	8	9	10
Leftwich, J. W.	Tenn.	D.	A	X	X	O	X	X		O	O	X	X
Loan, B. F.	Mo.	R.	O	O	O	X	O	X		O	O	O	O
Longyear, J. W.	Mich.	R.	A	O	O	X	O	O		X	X	O	O
Lynch, John	Me.	R.	O	O	O	X	O	O		O	X	O	O
Marshall, S. S.	Ill.	D.	A	X	A	X	O	X		O	O	X	X
Marston, Gilman	N.H.	R.	A	O	A	X	O	O		X	A	A	A
Marvin, J. M.	N.Y.	R.	A	X	X	O	X	O		X	X	X	O
Maynard, Horace	Tenn.	R.	O	A	O	X	O	O		X	X	O	O
McClurg, J. W.	Mo.	R.	O	O	O	O	O	O		O	O	O	O
McCullough, Hiram	Md.	D.	A	A	A	A	A	A		O	O	X	X
McIndoe, W. D.	Wisc.	R.	A	A	O	A	A	A		X	X	O	O
McKee, Samuel	Ky.	R.	O	X	X	O	X	O		X	O	X	O
McRuer, D. C.	Calif.	R.	O	X	O	O	X	O		X	X	X	O
Mercur, Ulysses	Penn.	R.	O	O	O	O	O	O		O	X	O	O
Miller, G. F.	Penn.	R.	O	A	O	O	O	O		X	X	X	O
Moorhead, J. K.	Penn.	R.	O	X	A	O	O	O		X	X	X	O
Morrill, J. S.	Vt.	R.	O	O	A	O	X	O		A	A	A	A
Morris, Daniel	N.Y.	R.	O	A	O	X	X	O		X	X	O	O
Moulton, S. W.	Ill.	D.	O	X	O	X	O	O		O	X	O	O
Myers, Leonard	Penn.	R.	O	O	O	X	O	O		O	X	O	O
Newell, W. A.	N.J.	R.	O	O	O	X	O	O		O	X	O	O
Niblack, W. E.	Ind.	D.	X	X	X	X	O	X		O	O	X	X
Nicholson, J. A.	Del.	D.	X	X	X	O	X	X		O	O	X	X
Noell, T. E.	Mo.	D.	X	X	X	X	X	X		A	A	X	X
O'Neill, Charles	Penn.	R.	O	O	O	X	O	O		O	X	O	O
Orth, G. S.	Ind.	R.	O	O	O	X	O	O		X	A	O	O
Paine, H. E.	Wisc.	R.	O	O	O	X	O	O		O	X	O	O
Patterson, J. W.	N.H.	R.	O	X	O	O	X	O		X	X	O	O
Perham, Sidney	Me.	R.	O	O	O	X	O	O		O	X	O	O
Phelps, C. E.	Md.	D.	X	A	X	O	X	A		O	O	X	X
Pike, F. A.	Me.	R.	O	O	O	X	O	O		O	A	O	O
Plants, T. A.	Ohio	R.	O	X	X	O	X	O		X	A	O	O
Pomeroy, T. M.	N.Y.	R.	O	X	A	A	A	A		X	X	X	O
Price, Hiram	Iowa	R.	O	O	O	O	X	O		X	X	O	O
Radford, William	N.Y.	D.	A	A	X	O	O	X		O	A	X	X

Vote on Roll Calls

Representative	State	Party	1	2	3	4	5	6	7	8	9	10
Randall, S. J.	Penn.	D.	X	X	A	O	X	X	O	O	X	X
Randall, W. H.	Ky.	R.	A	X	X	O	X	X	A	O	A	A
Raymond, H. J.	N.Y.	R.	X	X	X	O	X	X	X	X	X	O
Rice, A. H.	Mass.	R.	O	X	O	O	A	O	X	X	O	O
Rice, J. H.	Me.	R.	O	X	A	O	X	O	X	A	X	O
Ritter, B. C.	Ky.	D.	X	X	X	O	O	X	O	O	X	X
Rogers, A. J.	N.J.	D.	X	X	X	X	O	X	O	A	X	X
Rollins, E. H.	N.H.	R.	O	O	O	X	O	O	X	X	O	O
Ross, L. W.	Ill.	D.	A	X	X	O	O	X	O	O	X	X
Rousseau, L. H.	Ky.	D.	X	A	X	O	X	X	X	A	X	X
Sawyer, Philetus	Wisc.	R.	A	O	O	X	O	O	O	X	O	O
Schenck, R. C.	Ohio	R.	O	X	X	O	X	O	X	X	O	O
Scofield, Glenni	Penn.	R.	O	O	O	X	O	O	O	O	O	O
Shanklin, G. S.	Ky.	D.	X	X	X	X	A	X	O	O	X	X
Shellabarger, Samuel	Ohio	R.	O	O	O	X	O	O	O	X	O	O
Sitgreaves, Charles	N.J.	D.	X	X	X	A	X	X	O	A	X	X
Sloan, I. C.	Wisc.	R.	O	O	O	X	O	O	O	X	O	O
Spalding, R. P.	Ohio	R.	X	X	O	X	O	O	X	A	O	O
Starr, J. F.	N.J.	R.	O	O	O	X	O	O	O	X	O	O
Stevens, Thaddeus	Penn.	R.	O	O	O	X	O	O	O	O	O	O
Stillwell, T. N.	Ind.	R.	X	A	X	O	X	X	X	A	X	A
Stokes, W. B.	Tenn.	R.	O	O	O	X	O	O	O	X	O	O
Strouse, Myer	Penn.	D.	X	X	X	X	X	X	O	A	X	X
Taber, Stephen	N.Y.	D.	X	X	X	X	O	X	O	O	X	X
Taylor, N. G.	Tenn.	D.	A	X	X	O	X	X	X	O	X	X
Taylor, Nelson	N.Y.	D.	X	X	X	O	X	X	O	O	X	X
Thayer, M. R.	Penn.	R.	O	A	X	O	X	O	X	X	X	O
Thomas, Francis	Md.	R.	A	O	X	X	X	X	X	X	A	O
Thomas, J. L., Jr.	Md.	R.	A	O	A	O	X	X	X	X	A	O
Thornton, Anthony	Ill.	D.	A	X	X	X	O	X	O	A	X	X
Trimble, L. S.	Ky.	D.	X	X	A	A	A	A	O	O	X	X
Trowbridge, R. E.	Mich.	R.	O	O	O	X	O	O	O	O	O	O
Upson, Charles	Mich.	R.	O	O	O	X	O	O	X	X	O	O
Van Aernam, Henry	N.Y.	R.	O	O	O	X	O	O	O	X	O	O
Van Horn, Burt	N.Y.	R.	A	X	O	X	O	O	X	X	O	O

Vote on Roll Calls

Representative	State	Party	1	2	3	4	5	6	7	8	9	10
Van Horn, R. T.	Mo.	R.	O	O	X	X	O	O	O	O	O	O
Ward, A. H.	Ky.	D.	X	X	X	O	O	X	O	O	X	X
Ward, Hamilton	N.Y.	R.	O	O	O	X	O	O	O	A	O	O
Warner, S. L.	Conn.	R.	O	X	O	X	X	O	O	X	O	O
Washburn, H. D.	Ind.	R.	O	X	A	A	A	A	A	A	O	O
Washburn, W. B.	Mass.	R.	O	X	O	O	O	O	X	X	O	O
Washburne, E. B.	Ill.	R.	O	A	A	A	A	A	A	A	A	A
Welker, Martin	Ohio	R.	A	X	A	O	O	O	X	X	O	O
Wentworth, John	Ill.	R.	O	O	O	X	O	O	O	A	O	O
Whaley, K. V.	W.Va.	R.	A	X	X	O	X	O	X	O	X	O
Williams, Thomas	Penn.	R.	O	A	A	X	O	O	O	O	O	O
Wilson, J. F.	Iowa	R.	O	O	O	O	X	O	X	X	O	O
Wilson, S. F.	Penn.	R.	O	O	O	X	O	O	O	O	O	O
Windom, William	Minn.	R.	O	O	X	X	O	O	O	O	O	O
Winfield, Charles	N.Y.	D.	A	X	A	A	A	A	A	A	X	X
Woodbridge, F. E.	Vt.	R.	A	X	O	O	X	O	X	X	O	O
Wright, E. R. V.	N.J.	D.	O	X	A	A	A	A	O	O	X	X

IV

Membership of
Republican Factions During 2nd Session
of 39th Congress (1866–67)

Congressman and State	Percentage of Votes Received in Election of				
	1862	1863	1864	1865	1866*
Ultra Radicals (12)					
Ashley, J. M. (Ohio)	38.5		51.8		53.4
Baxter, Portus (Vt.)		73.0	74.1		
Bidwell, John (Calif.)			55.8		
Clarke, R. W. (Ohio)			55.3		53.0
Cook, B. C. (Ill.)			60.9		66.0
Dixon, N. F. (R.I.)		56.9		69.0	
Donnelly, Ignatius (Minn.)	58.5		56.9		60.7
Dumont, Ebenezer (Ind.)	53.3		63.4		
Hayes, R. B. (Ohio)			58.7		56.2
McClurg, J. W. (Mo.)	53.2		73.1		65.0
Mercur, Ulysses (Penn.)			52.7		52.8
Miller, G. F. (Penn.)			51.1		52.8

	1862	1863	1864	1865	1866
Stevens Radicals (47)					
Alley, J. B. (Mass.)	61.1		75.8		
Arnell, S. M. (Tenn.)				45.5	
Barker, A. A. (Penn.)			51.4		
Beaman, F. C. (Mich.)	50.3		53.4		56.2
Boutwell, G. S. (Mass.)	55.1		68.9		77.3
Bromwell, H. P. H. (Ill.)			56.0		56.7
Clarke, Sidney (Kans.)			54.0		70.3
Cobb, Amasa (Wisc.)	56.3		63.6		62.9
Cullom, S. M. (Ill.)			52.9		56.1
Driggs, J. F. (Mich.)	51.7		54.0		58.0
Eckley, E. R. (Ohio)	52.4		59.3		
Eliot, T. D. (Mass.)	75.2		82.7		84.1
Grinnell, J. B. (Iowa)	52.8		61.4		
Harding, A. C. (Ill.)			51.6		54.3
Henderson, J. H. D. (Ore.)			59.2		
Higby, William (Calif.)	n.a.		61.3		52.0
Holmes, S. T. (N.Y.)			59.9		
Hubbard, J. H. (Conn.)		50.8		56.3	
Julian, G. W. (Ind.)	55.5		68.7		65.1
Kelley, W. D. (Penn.)	52.4		58.3		54.5
Koontz, W. H. (Penn.)			50.1		51.1
Longyear, J. W. (Mich.)	51.7		54.7		
Lynch, John (Me.)			54.5		57.2
Marston, Gilman (N.H.)				55.8	
Maynard, Horace (Tenn.)				55.9	
Myers, Leonard (Penn.)	50.1		53.4		52.0
Newell, W. A. (N.J.)			50.1		
O'Neill, Charles (Penn.)	58.6		61.7		57.1
Orth, G. S. (Ind.)	51.8		52.2		50.3
Paine, H. E. (Wisc.)			51.0		58.7
Perham, Sidney (Me.)	56.9		60.5		65.1
Pike, F. A. (Me.)	52.7		58.6		60.7
Rollins, E. H. (N.H.)		50.8		55.2	
Sawyer, Philetus (Wisc.)			56.2		60.5
Scofield, Glenni (Penn.)	51.2		53.7		54.7

	1862	1863	1864	1865	1866
Shellabarger, Samuel (Ohio)			57.0		54.3
Sloan, I. C. (Wisc.)	54.6		60.7		
Starr, J. F. (N.J.)	51.4		54.4		
Stevens, Thaddeus (Penn.)	62.5		61.6		62.2
Stokes, W. B. (Tenn.)				56.6	
Trowbridge, R. E. (Mich.)			53.3		54.6
Upson, Charles (Mich.)	55.4		60.4		63.6
Van Aernam, Henry (N.Y.)			65.4		66.3
Ward, Hamilton (N.Y.)			60.2		60.8
Wentworth, John (Ill.)			56.5		
Williams, Thomas (Penn.)	54.0		58.9		
Wilson, S. F. (Penn.)			51.9		53.7
Independent Radicals (13)					
Allison, W. B. (Iowa)	58.8		60.3		59.6
Anderson, G. W. (Mo.)			51.8		50.9
Baldwin, J. D. (Mass.)	66.1		74.8		82.6
Blow, H. T. (Mo.)	69.5		83.1		
Broomall, J. M. (Penn.)	60.5		60.1		58.4
Eggleston, Benjamin (Ohio)			56.9		52.3
Farquhar, J. H. (Ind.)			50.1		
Moorhead, J. K. (Penn.)	58.6		61.5		56.8
Morrill, J. S. (Vt.)		70.3	72.1		
Price, Hiram (Iowa)	58.1		65.2		63.8
Washburn, W. B. (Mass.)	100.0		81.4		87.0
Welker, Martin (Ohio)			55.4		53.3
Wilson, J. F. (Iowa)	54.7		65.1		60.9
Moderates (33, including 1 Democrat)					
Ashley, D. R. (Nev.)			n.a.		54.0
Bingham, J. A. (Ohio)			52.6		52.8
Blaine, J. G. (Me.)	60.3		59.0		64.2
Buckland, R. P. (Ohio)			53.5		52.2
Bundy, H. S. (Ohio)			59.7		
Darling, W. A. (N.Y.)			38.8		
Dawes, H. L. (Mass.)	56.2		64.7		66.0

	1862	1863	1864	1865	1866
Delano, Columbus (Ohio)			50.4		49.4
Deming, H. C. (Conn.)		50.8		57.0	
Farnsworth, J. F. (Ill.)	72.4		77.3		82.8
Ferry, T. W. (Mich.)			58.9		65.2
Garfield, J. A. (Ohio)	66.2		74.1		71.3
Hill, Ralph (Ind.)			51.8		
Hooper, Samuel (Mass.)	52.2		64.0		71.2
Ingersoll, E. C. (Ill.)			61.6		65.6
Jenckes, T. A. (R.I.)		58.5		99.0	
Ketcham, J. H. (N.Y.)			51.4		53.6
Laflin, A. H. (N.Y.)			56.4		58.4
Lawrence, G. V. (Penn.)			53.6		53.0
Lawrence, William (Ohio)			56.1		54.6
Marvin, J. M. (N.Y.)	51.0		51.5		55.6
McKee, Samuel (Ky.)				56.6	
McRuer, D. C. (Calif.)			58.2		
Moulton, S. W. (Ill.), *Democrat*					
Patterson, J. W. (N.H.)		50.6		56.2	
Plants, T. A. (Ohio)			57.3		54.3
Rice, A. H. (Mass.)	50.1		62.3		
Rice, J. H. (Me.)	60.6		60.7		
Schenck, R. C. (Ohio)	52.5		55.3		51.8
Thayer, M. R. (Penn.)	50.1		50.6		
Van Horn, Burt (N.Y.)			57.0		57.2
Whaley, K. V. (W.Va.)			n.a.		
Woodbridge, F. E. (Vt.)		71.0	72.0		77.6
Conservatives (13)					
Baker, Jehu (Ill.)			50.1		52.1
Banks, N. P. (Mass.)				80.0	74.9
Davis, T. T. (N.Y.)	58.4		58.5		
Defrees, J. H. (Ind.)			51.0		
Dodge, W. E. (N.Y.)			39.1		
Kelso, J. R. (Mo.)			49.3		
Kuykendall, A. J. (Ill.)			52.1		

	1862	1863	1864	1865	1866
Loan, B. F. (Mo.)	43.5		81.1		73.2
Randall, W. H. (Ky.)		97.5		76.3	
Raymond, H. J. (N.Y.)			42.4		
Stillwell, T. N. (Ind.)			53.8		
Thomas, Francis (Md.)		100.0	61.1		54.8
Thomas, J. L., Jr. (Md.)				83.1	

Republicans not clearly identified with any faction 8

	1862	1863	1864	1865	1866
Hubbard, C. D. (W.Va.)			n.a.		54.8
Hubbell, J. R. (Ohio)			54.8		
Hulburd, C. T. (N.Y.)	67.1		69.9		72.4
Morris, Daniel (N.Y.)	58.7		58.7		
Spalding, R. P. (Ohio)	68.8		68.4		64.4
Van Horn, R. T. (Mo.)			46.5		56.6
Warner, S. L. (Conn.)				54.8	
Windom, William (Minn.)	57.4		60.5		63.5

Republicans not voting on 4 or more of 6 test roll calls

	1862	1863	1864	1865	1866
Ames, Oakes (Mass.)	61.1		72.0		79.5
Benjamin, J. F. (Mo.)			74.1		55.6
Brandegee, Augustus (Conn.)		58.1			
Colfax, Schuyler (Ind.), *Speaker*	50.3		52.6		52.8
Conkling, Roscoe (N.Y.)			52.5		53.0
Culver, C. V. (Penn.)			52.7		
Griswold, J. A. (N.Y.)			54.1		60.1
Hale, R. S. (N.Y.)				54.4	
Hart, Roswell (N.Y.)			52.4		
Hotchkiss, G. W. (N.Y.)	58.6		58.9		
Hubbard, A. W. (Iowa)	66.1		72.7		71.7
Hubbard, Demas, Jr. (N.Y.)			54.7		
Kasson, J. A. (Iowa)	58.3		65.7		
McIndoe, W. D. (Wisc.)	58.1		66.5		

	1862	1863	1864	1865	1866
Pomeroy, T. M. (N.Y.)	55.2		57.5		58.6
Washburn, H. D. (Ind.)			50.0		50.8
Washburne, E. B. (Ill.)	60.7		67.9		71.3

*"n.a." indicates that election returns are not available.